UNLOCKING THE SECRETS OF
BITCOIN & CRYPTOCURRENCY

Crypto Currency Made Easy

Sir Patrick Bijou

UNLOCKING THE SECRETS OF BITCOIN CRYPTOCURRENCY

Crypto Currency Made Easy

By

Sir Patrick Bijou

UNLOCKING THE SECERETS OF BITCOIN CRYPTOCURRENCY

ISBN 978-1-9993023-1-3

TABLE OF CONTENTS

CHAPTER THREE

CHAPTER FOUR

CHAPTER 5

CHAPTER ONE

INTRODUCTION

Technology has come to a new level – from digital phones, tablets, computers, and now the Digital Currency also known as Cryptocurrency of the new generation. Many people use debit and credit cards instead of a physical money coming from their pocket wallets to pay for their purchases, but there is more than just a card to pay for your commodities at this millennium, and it is actually 'Cryptocurrency'.Not everyone knows what cryptocurrency is, some even think that it is a scam, some people think it's not true until they know how it is done.

There are many types of cryptocurrency, Bitcoin or BTC is the most popular especially for beginners. Next to bitcoin is the Ethereum, Litecoin, Ripple, Dash, IOTA, Monero, Zcash Zcash, Cardano, Stellar, NEM, NEO and Tron. The said cryptocurrencies have their sorts of similarities and differences, when it comes to uses, trading, and policies. Japan has officially open its door for digital currencies as a means of payment next to real money. Japan and South Korea drives a high traffic of cryptocurrency exchanges according to CoinMarketCap, in fact South Korea is making major improvements as of 2017 for more safety transactions in the Bitcoin World.

Some say that cryptocurrencies tend to be bad because of their bubble like characteristic. There are also people who find it very useful, in fact, many make money from it while in the four corners of their homes. There are lots of merchandisers and big companies that are now accepting virtual money as a form of payment for every purchase. Booking flight and buying software online is also covered by virtual money, you can now book flights and purchase software from Microsoft using Bitcoins with hassle free transaction.

What is Crypto Currency?

A cryptocurrency is a medium of exchange like normal currencies such as USD, but designed for the purpose of exchanging digital information through a process made possible by certain principles of cryptography. Cryptography is used to secure the transactions and to control the creation of new coins.

Why Crypto Currency?

Money exists to facilitate trade. Through the centuries trade has become incredibly complex everyone trades with everyone worldwide. Trade is recorded in book keeping, this information is often isolated and closed to the public. This is the reason why we use third parties and middlemen we trust to facilitate and approve our transactions. Think governments, banks, accountants, notaries and the paper money in your wallet. We call these trusted third parties. Cryptocurrency software enables a network of computers to maintain a collective bookkeeping via the internet. This bookkeeping is neither closed nor in control of one party or a central authority. Rather, it is public, and available in one digital ledger which is fully distributed across the network. We call this the blockchain. In the blockchain all the transactions are logged, including information on the time, date, participants and amount of every single transaction. Each node in the network owns a full copy of the blockchain. On the basis of complicated state-of-the-art mathematical principles the transactions are verified by the cryptocurrency miners, whom maintain the ledger. The mathematical principles also ensure that these nodes automatically and continuously agree about the current state of the ledger and every transaction in it. If anyone attempts to corrupt transaction the nodes will not arrive at a consensus and hence will refuse to incorporate the transaction in the blockchain. So every transaction is public and thousands of nodes unanimously agreed that a transaction has occurred on date X at time Y. It's almost like there's a notary present at every transaction. This way everyone has access to a shared single source of truth. The ledger does not care whether a cryptocurrency represents a certain amount of Euros or Dollars, or anything else of value, or property for that matter. Users can decide for themselves what a unit of cryptocurrency represents. A cryptocurrency like Bitcoin is divisible in to 100 million units and each unit is both individually identifiable and programmable. This means that users can assign properties to each unit, users can program a unit to represent a Euro cent, or a share in a company, a kilowatt our energy or digital certificate of ownership. Because of if this cryptocurrencies and blockchain technology could be used for more than simply money and payments. A cryptocurrency can represent many kinds of property. A thousand barrels of oil, award credits or a vote during an election for example. Moreover cryptocurrency protocols allows us to make our currency smarter and to automize our cash and money flows. Imagine a health care allowance in dollars or Euros that can only be used to pay for health care at certified parties. In this case, whether someone actually follows the rules is no longer verified in the bureaucratic process afterwards. You simply program these rules into the money, compliance up front. The unit can even be programmed in such a way that it will automatically be returned to the provider if the receiver doesn't use it after a certain amount of time. This way the provider can ensure that allowances are not horded. A company can control its spending in the same way. By programming budgets for salaries machinery, materials and maintenance so that the respective money is specified and cannot be spent on other things. Automating such matters leads to considerable decrease in bureaucracy.

Bitcoin

Bitcoin is a new currency that was created in 2009 by an unknown person using the alias Satoshi Nakamoto. Transactions are made with no middle men – meaning, no banks! There are no transaction fees and no need to give your real name. More merchants are beginning to accept them. You can buy webhosting services, pizza or even Buy on an Exchange. Bitcoins are stored in a "digital wallet," which exists either in the cloud or on a user's computer. The wallet is a kind of virtual bank account that allows users to send or receive bitcoins, pay for goods or save their money. Unlike bank accounts, bitcoin wallets are not insured by the FDIC. Though each bitcoin transaction is recorded in a public log, names of buyers' and sellers are never revealed – only their wallet IDs. While that keeps bitcoin users' transactions private, it also lets them buy or sell anything without easily tracing it back to them. That's why it has become the currency of choice for people online buying drugs or other illicit activities.

Exchange Bitcoins:

Several marketplaces called "bitcoin exchanges" allow people to buy or sell bitcoins using different currencies. Mt. Gox is the largest bitcoin Transfer: People can send bitcoins to each other using mobile apps or their computers. It's similar to sending cash digitally.

The Technology Behind Bitcoin

On the surface, Bitcoin transactions appear to be fast and easy – and they truly are. However, behind the scenes, the technology that makes the Bitcoin network run seamlessly is a massive ledger known as the blockchain.

It's massive because it contains a record of all bitcoin transactions that have ever taken place since Bitcoin was first released in 2009.

As more time passes by and more transactions occur, the size of the blockchain will continue to grow. So here is how the blockchain works:

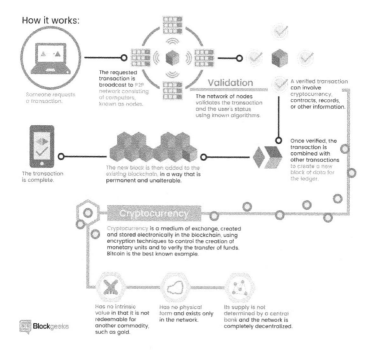

(Image Source: BlockGeeks.com)

Mining:

People compete to "mine" bitcoins using computers to solve complex math puzzles. This is how bitcoins are created. Currently, winner is rewarded with 25 bitcoins roughly every 10 minutes.

Symbol:

Ƀ is not a logo but a symbol: Unicode Character U+0243 can be used by Unicode text editor. This unicode character was originally used as a phonetic symbol to represent or transcribe the sound [β]. Thus the context of this use does not allow any confusion with the Bitcoin currency.

Unit:

One BTC is equal to mBTC 0.001 and 1 mBTC is equal to uBTC 0.000001 subsequently 1 uBTC is equal to 0.00000001 Satoshi's. Making Satoshi the least unit of the currency.

He is said to be from Japan but his mail ID was from Germany, plus the bitcoin software was not available in Japanese. He developed the system and the Bitcoin software (that is used to run the system) in 2009 but disappeared into thin air in 2010. The other developers of the system stopped hearing from him in 2010, and plenty of speculation turned up about his real identity. Some even suggested that his name was just a mashup of popular Japanese companies —

SAmsung TOSHIba NAKAmichi MOTOrola. But what he created was definitely the fantasy of every tech guy in the world.

2007, Satoshi Nakamoto

According to legend, Satoshi Nakamoto began working on the Bitcoin concept in 2007. While he is on record as living in Japan, it is speculated that Nakamoto may be a collective pseudonym for more than one person.

August 2008, An interesting patent application

Three individuals, Neal Kin, Vladimir Oksman, and Charles Bry file made an application for an encryption patent. All three individuals deny having any connection to Satoshi Nakamoto, the alleged originator of the Bitcoin concept. The three also register the site Bitcoin.org in the same month, over on anonymousspeech.com – which allows people to buy domain names anonymously.

October 2008, The White paper is published

Despite the above, Satoshi Nakamoto releases his white paper, revealing his idea for a purely peer-to-peer version of electronic cash to the world. In his vision, he manages to solve the problem of money being copied, providing a vital foundation for Bitcoin to grow legitimately.

November 9, 2008, The Bitcoin Project hits SourceForge

The Bitcoin project is registered on SourceForge.net, a community collaboration website focused on the development and distribution of open source software.

January 3, 2009, The Genesis Block is mined

The first block, nicknamed 'Genesis' is launched allowing the initial 'mining' of Bitcoins to take place. Later that month, the first transaction takes place between Satoshi and Hal Finney, a developer and cryptographic activist.

January 9, 2009, Version 0.1 is released

Version 0.1 of Bitcoin is released. Compiled with Microsoft Visual Studio for Windows, it lacks a command line interface and is so complete that it furthers speculation that it was developed by more than one person (or by an academic with little programming experience and a great deal of theoretical know-how). It includes a Bitcoin generation system that would create a total of 21 million Bitcoins through the year 2040.

January 12, 2009, The first Bitcoin transaction

The first transaction of Bitcoin currency, in block 170, takes place between Satoshi and Hal Finney, a developer and cryptographic activist.

October 5, 2009, An exchange rate is established

Bitcoin receives an equivalent value in traditional currencies. The New Liberty Standard established the value of a Bitcoin at $1 = 1,309 BTC. The equation was derived so as to include the cost of electricity to run the computer that created the Bitcoins in the first place.

Hong Kong's First Bitcoin Counter Opens To The Public October 12, 2009, #bitcoin-dev hits freenode IRC

The #bitcoin-dev channel is registered on freenode IRC, a discussion network for free and open source development communities.

December 16, 2009, Version 0.2 is released

Version 0.2 of Bitcoin is released.

December 30, 2009, The difficulty increases

The first difficulty increase occurs at 06:11:04 GMT.

February 6, 2010, A currency exchange is born

The world's first Bitcoin market is established by the now defunct dwdollar.

February 18, 2010, Encryption patent is published

The encryption patent application that was filed on August 15, 2008 by Neal Kin, Vladimir Oksman, and Charles Bry was published.

May 22, 2010, 10,000 BTC spent on pizza

A programmer living in Florida named Laslo Hanyecz sends 10,000BTC to a volunteer in England, who spent about $25 to order Hanyecz a pizza from Papa John's. Today that pizza is valued at £1,961,034 and stands as a major milestone in Bitcoin's history.

July 7, 2010, Version 0.3 released

Version 0.3 of Bitcoin is released.

July 11, 2010, Slashdot drives surge in Bitcoin users.

Mention of Bitcoin v0.3 on slashdot brings in a large number of new Bitcoin users.

July 12, 2010, Bitcoin value increases tenfold

Over a five day period beginning on July 12, the exchange value of Bitcoin increases ten times from US\$0.008/BTC to US\$0.080/BTC.

July 17, 2010, MtGox is established

The MtGox Bitcoin currency exchange market is established by Jed McCaleb.

July 18, 2010, OpenGL GPU hash farm and ArtForz

ArtForz establishes an OpenGL GPU hash farm and generates his first Bitcoin block.

August 15,2010, Exploit generates 184 billion Bitcoins

Bitcoin is hacked. A vulnerability in how the system verifies the value of Bitcoin is discovered, leading to the generation of 184 billion Bitcoins. The value of the currency – from a high of \$0.80 to \$1 in June drops through the floor.

September 14, 2010, An offer for CUDA

An offer is made by jgarzik, in the name of the Bitcoin Store, to puddinpop to open source their Windows-based CUDA client. The offer was in the form of 10,000 BTC which, at the time, was valued at around US$600 to US$650.

September 14, 2010, Block 79,764

Split allocation of the generation reward used to mine Block 79,764.

September 18, 2010, CUDA becomes open-source

Under the MIT license, puddinpop releases the source of their Windows-based CUDA client, open sourced by the Bitcoin Store, following a contribution by jgarzik.

September 18, 2010, Slush's Pool mines its first block

Bitcoin Pooled Mining (operated by slush), a method by which several users work collectively to mine Bitcoins and share in the benefits, mines its first block.

September 29, 2010, Another exploit discovered

A microtransactions exploit is discovered by kermit, precipitating the release of Version 0.3.13.

October 2010 Financial task force issues warning

Bitcoin goes under the spotlight. After the hack in August – and a subsequent discovery of other vulnerabilities in the blockchain in September – an inter-governmental group publishes a report on money laundering using new payment methods. Bitcoin, it suggested could help people finance terrorist groups.

October 7, 2010, Stalled Bitcoin value begins climb

The Bitcoin exchange rate, stalled at US$0.06/BTC for several months, begins to climb.

October 10, 2010, MtGox switches to Liberty Reserve

MtGox changes its main funding option from PayPal to Liberty Reserve.

October 16, 2010, First escrow transaction takes place

Bitcoin Forum members Diablo-D3 and nanotube conduct the first recorded escrow trade of Bitcoins with theymos as escrow.

October 17, 2010, #bitcoin-otc trading channel opens

The #bitcoin-otc trading channel is registered on freenode IRC as a marketplace for over-the-counter trading of Bitcoins.

October 28, 2010, First ever short sale

Facilitated by #bitcoin-otc, the first recorded short sale of Bitcoins is initiated in the form of a 100 BTC loan from nanotube to kiba.

November 6, 2010

Bitcoin reaches $1 million. Based on the number of Bitcoins in circulation at the time, the valuation leads to a surge in Bitcoin value to $0.50/BTC

December 7, 2010, Bitcoind compiled for Nokia N900

Bitcoin Forum member doublec compiles Bitcoind, which was written for the Nokia N900 mobile computer.

December 8, 2010, First mobile Bitcoin transaction

The first portable-to-portable transaction of Bitcoins occurs when ribuck sends doublec 0.42 BTC using bitcoin.

December 9, 2010, First call option contract sold

The first call option contract for Bitcoins is sold on the #bitcoin-otc market. The transaction occurs between nanotube and sgomick.

December 9, 2010, Difficulty increases

The generation difficulty exceeds 10,000

January 2011, Silk Road opens for business

The Silk Road, an illicit drugs marketplace is established, using Bitcoin as an untraceable way to buy and sell drugs online.

January 2, 2011, Tonal Bitcoin standardizes its units

Tonal Bitcoin, designed for those who prefer the Tonal number system, standardizes its units.

February 2011, Bitcoin reaches parity with US dollar

Bitcoin reaches parity with the US dollar for the first time. By June each Bitcoin is worth $31 giving the currency a market cap of $206 million.

February 14, 2011, Vehicle offered for Bitcoins

An Australian member of the Bitcoin Forum attempts to sell his 1984 Celica Supra for 3000 BTC, and becomes the first person to offer a vehicle in exchange for Bitcoins.

February 25, 2011, WeUseCoins.com is created

WeUseCoins.com is registered and built into a Bitcoin resource and creates one of the most watched videos on Bitcoin.

April 23, 2011, Bitcoin passes parity with Euro

On MtGox, the BTC/USD exchange rate reaches and passes parity with the Euro and the British Sterling Pound. The value of Bitcoin money stock passes US$10 million.

June 13, 2011, Largest ever Bitcoin theft reported

The first major theft takes place. Bitcoin Forum founder allinvain reports having 25,000 BTC taken from his digital wallet, which had an equivalent value of $375,000. In the same month, a major breach of security sees the value of the currency go from $17.51 to $0.01 per Bitcoin.

June 2012, Coinbase is founded

Coinbase, a bitcoin wallet and platform, is founded in San Francisco, California.

November 15, 2012, WordPress.com accepts Bitcoin

WordPress.com announces that it accepts Bitcoins as a form of payment for users to purchase upgrades.

November 28, 2012, Halving Day

On Halving Day, Block 210,000 is the first with a block reward subsidy of 25 BTC.

March 18, 2013, FinCEN defines stance on Bitcoin

The US Financial Crimes Enforcement Network (FINCEN) issues some of the world's first bitcoin regulation in the form of a guidance report for persons administering, exchanging or using virtual currency. This marked the beginning of an ongoing debate on how best to regulate bitcoin.

March 28, 2013, Market cap reaches $1 billion

Bitcoin market capitalisation reaches $1bn.

May 2, 2013, First Bitcoin ATM unveiled

The first Bitcoin ATM in the world is debuted in San Diego, California.

May 18, 2013, PrimeDice.com launches online casino

PrimeDice.com launches as an online casino platform that accepts Bitcoin wager

August 20,2013, Bitcoin ruled private money in Germany

Federal Judge Mazzant claims: "It is clear that Bitcoin can be used as money" and "It can be used to purchase goods or services" in a case against Trendon Shavers, the so-called 'Bernie Madoff of bitcoin'. Bloomberg begins testing bitcoin data on its terminal. Although alternative tickers exist, endorsement from Bloomberg gives bitcoin more institutional legitimacy.

November 2013, The US Senate holds its first hearings on the digital currency

Bitcoin price climbs to $700 in as the US Senate holds its first hearings on the digital currency. The Federal Reserve chairman at the time, Ben Bernanke, gives his blessing to bitcoin. In his letter to the Senate homeland security and government affairs committee, Bernanke states that bitcoin "may hold long-term promise, particularly if the innovations promote a faster, more secure and more efficient payment system".

December 2013, China's Central Bank bans Bitcoin transactions

China's central bank bars financial institutions from handling bitcoin transactions. This ban was issued after the People's Bank of China said bitcoin is not a currency with "real meaning" and does not have the same legal status as fiat currency. The ban reflects the risk bitcoin poses to China's capital controls and financial stability. Today China remains the world's biggest bitcoin trader, with 80% of global bitcoin transactions being processed in China.

January 2014, First insured bitcoin storage service

Bitcoin custodians Elliptic launch the world's first insured bitcoin storage service for institutional clients. All deposits are comprehensively insured by a Fortune 100 insurer and held in full reserve. This means Elliptic never re-invests client assets; instead they secure them in deep cold storage. Overstock.com becomes the first major online retailer to embrace bitcoin, accepting payments in the US. Overstock was the first in what is now an expeditiously growing list of large businesses that accept bitcoin.

February 2014, HMRC classifies bitcoin as assets

HMRC classifies bitcoin as assets or private money, meaning that no VAT will be charged on the mining or exchange of bitcoin. This is important as it is the world's first and most progressive treatment of bitcoin, positioning the

UK government as the most forward thinking and comprehensive with regard to bitcoin taxation.

June 2014, The illegal online marketplace

The US government auctions off more than 29,000 bitcoins seized from the Silk Road, the illegal online marketplace. The sale and closure of the marketplace marks growing institutional understanding of the potential use cases of bitcoin. Additionally, the closure and auction of the Silk Road has helped bitcoin gain legitimacy as it demonstrates that bitcoin is not an easy way for online criminals to avoid the rule of law.

From this point onwards, bitcoin can no longer be considered as a currency for criminals. The use of the bitcoin blockchain means that the identity of users can often be established.

July 2014, 'Bit Licence'

The 'Bit Licence' edges towards reality as the New York State Department of Financial Services releases the first draft of the agency's proposed rules for regulating virtual currencies. The

European Banking Authority publishes its opinion on 'virtual currencies'. Their analytical report recommends that EU legislators consider declaring virtual currency exchanges as 'obliged entities' must comply with anti-money laundering (AML) and counter-terrorist financing requirements.

The EBA report is important as it acts as a catalyst to launch bitcoin into the financial mainstream by highlighting the fact that virtual currencies require a regulatory approach to strive for an international coordination to achieve a successful regulatory regime. Also that month GABI (Global Advisors Bitcoin Investment Fund) launches the world's first regulated Bitcoin Investment fund. This is important to the bitcoin ecosystem as the launch of this investment vehicle adds further legitimacy to bitcoin in addition to allowing regulated investors a way to invest in bitcoin.

August 2014, HM Treasury's positive outlook on bitcoin

The Chancellor of the Exchequer, George Osborne, demonstrates his and HM Treasury's positive outlook on bitcoin when he purchases £20 worth of bitcoin and announces HM Treasury's Call for Information on digital currencies, offering digital currency businesses the chance to comment on the risks and benefits and potentially influence future government policy.

October 2014, TeraExchange

TeraExchange announces that the first bitcoin derivative transaction was executed on a regulated exchange, adding a new hedging instrument to bitcoin and instilling credibility and institutional confidence in the entire bitcoin community.

December 2014, Microsoft accept bitcoin

Tech giant Microsoft begins accepting bitcoin payments.

January 2015, NYSE

The New York Stock Exchange is a minority investor in Coinbase's $75M funding round. The

NYSE aims to tap into the new asset class by bringing transparency, security and confidence to bitcoin.

March 2015, UK Treasury's call

The results of the UK Treasury's call for information on digital currency are announced.

Future predictions

There are several possible ways Bitcoin can go at this point, all of which point to a legitimate, widespread adoption by large institutions through tighter regulation. Recently, New York's BitLicense became the world's first digital currency-specific regulatory regime. It has been through a couple of rounds of consultations and is expected to come into force in a couple of weeks.

The European Central Bank and European Banking authority have both released detailed reports on digital currencies, and suggested regulation of the industry by the EU to further control price fluctuations. The Winklevoss brothers, they of Facebook fame, are on the verge of launching their own exchange-traded fund holding Bitcoins.

Bitcoin's journey into the financial mainstream has already begun, with HM Treasury's report on digital currencies marking encouraging progress toward the predictions in this infographic. The report introduces anti-money laundering, consumer protection and technical standardisation for digital currency companies in the UK, which will encourage traditional financial services to engage more with digital currency businesses and accelerate the integration of blockchain technology within financial services.

THINGS TO KNOW ABOUT BITCOIN

Special About the Bitcoin System:

The Bitcoin is a system which allows you to do anonymous currency transactions and no one will come to know about the payment or about information related to the payment, including who sent it, who received it, etc.

Satoshi did it by making the system – a peer-to-peer network – controlled by no central authority but run by a network of contributors and freedom enthusiasts, who donated their time and energy to this innovation. Essentially, people can do money transactions and no authority or organization will come to know about it. Satoshi Nakamoto was so talented that he even solved the problem of double spending of digital currency in his system

Double Spending:

We can make many copies of digital data, e.g. people copy software and sell it as counterfeit or pirated copies. We may face the same problem with digital currency – one can copy the digital currency (let's suppose USD100) and use it as many time as he/she like (as many notes of USD100). Satoshi solved this problem by showing all transactions in a public list. Whenever a new transaction is made, its validity is checked by confirming from the list that the digital currency was not used before. This way, no one can copy the currency and use it for more than one time. It's a simple but effective idea to stop double spending of the same bitcoin.

Anonymity:

The public listing only shows the transaction ID and the amount of currency transferred. You will be anonymous in the system because you don't need to provide any of your personal details like your name, address, email, phone number, etc. In comparison, when you use payment gateways like Paypal you have to give up all these personal details.

Using of Bitcoin:

Bitcoins are kept in a digital wallet which you can keep in your computer, or on a website online, which will manage and secure your wallet for you. You can have as many wallets and bitcoin addresses (where you receive money from others) as you like. What's more, you can use Bitcoin software on top of Tor to prevent anyone from tracking your IP address – total anonymity guaranteed!

Total Bitcoins:

At this very moment, 10.71 million Bitcoins are in existence, which is like 207.929 million USD worth! In fact, the Canadian government is working on their own crypto-currency, named MintChip. (a glance:)

Mintchip, in one day, more than 45,000 transactions of a total of BTC 2.5 million (worth of USD48.5 million) is handled by the bitcoin network.

Spend Bitcoins:

Spending Bitcoins is a bit easier. You can send Bitcoins to a person, buy goods, or donate to non-profit foundations who accept it, such as Wikileaks, P2P Foundation, Operation Anonymous, Free Software Foundation, Archive.org.

You can send Bitcoins to anyone once you know their bitcoin address.

For merchandise, you can buy products from merchants that accept Bitcoins. Example – BitcoinDeals.

Bitcoin and transparency

ALTERNATIVES TO BITCOIN

Best Alternatives

Litecoin

Of all the competing cryptocurrencies, Litecoin is the most similar to Bitcoin. It has been thought of as silver to Bitcoin's gold, or MasterCard to Bitcoin's Visa. It has also managed to gain the second-highest market capitalization amongst digital currencies. One key difference includes a different hashing algorithm designed so that mining Litecoins won't result in a similar hardware arms race to the one Bitcoin is currently involved in. Litecoin mining these days involves rigs of video cards, or GPUs. It's similar to how Bitcoin mining was a few years ago, until its ASICs (application-specific integrated circuits) were designed from the ground up to mine Bitcoins. Litecoins also feature faster confirmation times due to shorter and faster block rewards. It's scheduled to produce 84 million Litecoins, four times as much as Bitcoin's 21 million.

Peercoin

Peercoin's distinguishing feature is that is uses a method called proof of stake as part of its mining, or as Peercoiners often like to say, "minting." Proof-of-stake rewards minters for the Peercoins they hold over time. This is measured in "coin days," one coin day being equivalent to holding one coin for one day. It's similar to how a kilowatt hour is defined as using a kilowatt over the course of one hour. So the more coins you hold over a longer time, the more Peercoins you receive through minting. This is in contrast to most cryptocurrencies' proof-of-work mining, which rewards miners based on how much computing power they contribute to keeping track of transactions. Peercoin also uses proof-of-work mining in conjunction with proof-of-work minting, although Peercoin is programmed to eventually rely only on proof-of-work mining. The maximum limit for the number of these coins is 2 billion. This is so much higher than Bitcoin's 21 million that it encourages inflationary pressure, which counterbalances the deflationary pressure caused by everyone trying to mint Peercoins and holding onto them.

NXT

Nxt is most similar to Peercoin in that is utilizes proof of stake to generate more coins. But unlike Peercoin, it uses proof of stake exclusively. The only way to get more Nxt coins is to hold them or exchange them in a process dubbed "forging," in contrast to Bitcoin mining and Peercoin minting. This has a "green" appeal in that it requires no massive, power-consuming hardware rigs, just a small program that will run on pretty much any modern computer. This also has the practical appeal of not requiring users to invest in the extra hardware and electricity. Instead, you merely exchange something for your initial Nxt coins. Nxt's developers also pride themselves on having written the Nxt code from scratch, while most alternative cryptocurrencies were developed from using Bitcoin's code as a basis.

Namecoin

Namecoin is similar to other cryptocurrencies, but with the additional feature of being a way to register domain names. Instead of .com or .net, Namecoin domain names have the .bit extension. Any method of registering and controlling a domain name is called a domain name system, or DNS. The current method of domain name registration is regulated by a nonprofit organization called the Internet Corporation for Assigned Names and Numbers, or ICANN. Because ICANN is a centralized organization, it ultimately has power over domain names and can shut down websites for political or other reasons. But because Namecoin is a decentralized network, no one is in control of it. Just like Bitcoin is a decentralized network that takes the power away from banks and other financial institutions, Namecoin is a decentralized network that takes the power away from ICANN or any other centralized DNS organization. Namecoin is also traded for its own sake, just like Bitcoin. It's just like any other cryptocurrency but with the added feature of a decentralized DNS system, which amounts to more "intrinsic value," which everyone is looking for.

Dogecoin

Dogecoin is a cryptocurrency inspired by the "Doge" Internet meme. Compared with the other cryptocurrencies, Doge is most similar to Litecoin. It uses scrypt, the same cryptographic function as Litecoin. A total of 100 billion Dogecoins will ever be mined, which is even more than Peercoin. Yet because the block reward is so large and frequent (every minute), Dogecoin miners have already mined almost 25 billion Dogecoins, almost 25% of the total. While Doge gets my vote for the best Internet meme of 2013, you would think that a cryptocurrency wouldn't manage to go far based on novelty. Yet Dogecoin's market capitalization is almost $7 million.

CHAPTER TWO

BITCOINS, WHAT THEY ARE AND HOW THEY WORK

What is a Bitcoin and how will Bitcoin change the way we do business around the world? Knowing the history of Bitcoin and how the currency works will help to understand how and to what extent Bitcoins will be essential to future financial progression. By the end of this and the coming chapters, the reader will understand the advantages and limitations of using a virtual currency.

For the purposes of this chapter, the definition of the European Central Bank of virtual currencies will be used: "A virtual currency is a type of unregulated, digital money, which is issued and usually controlled by its developers, and used and accepted among the members of a specific virtual community" (European Central Bank, 2012). The European Central Bank further specifies what virtual currencies are. It recognizes three types of virtual currency models, but I am most interested in what is referred to by the European Central Bank as Type Three virtual currencies. "Type Three virtual currencies have bidirectional flows, meaning that two exchange rates (buy and sell) exist, and they can be used to buy virtual goods and services, but also to purchase real goods and services."

Bitcoin was introduced in 2009, and created by a pseudonymous developer, Satoshi Nakamoto. Bitcoin uses open source software, which means that only the developer has the rights to make changes to the system (bitcoin.com). Bitcoin is a type of crypto-currency, which basically means that Bitcoin uses principles of cryptography to keep it secure. Cryptographers construct and develop protocols using mathematical equations that help to keep information and data confidential.

Bitcoins have a peer-to-peer payment system, peer-to-peer meaning that peers work together to make their networks available to one another without the need of a centralized server (bitcoin.org). A peer-to-peer payment system means that one person can transfer Bitcoins to another person without the interference of a bank. Technically, a Bitcoin is a series of hashtags combined with zeroes and ones, which are encrypted and stored on a hard drive of a computer or mobile device. "It may be best to think of its units being virtual tokens rather than physical coins or notes" (BBC, 2014).

Only twenty-one million Bitcoins can ever be in existence. This number was set up in the Bitcoin protocol (bitcoin.org). This Bitcoin protocol uses block chain transactions which controls and limits the ability of the user to double spend their Bitcoins. Specifically, block chain is a database that keeps track of ownership and any transactions (bitcoin.org). That being said, after a few years have passed, the number of Bitcoins to be rewarded will be cut in half. This means that the inflation rate of a Bitcoin can be controlled making the Bitcoin more desirable to users. It also ensures that Bitcoins will be around for a very long time.

According to the Bitcoin network, the protocol has been designed that develops the currency at a predictable rate. As time goes on, the mathematical equations to be solved become more difficult (more computing resources are needed). The Bitcoin website explains that the rate of creation will remain constant: six per hour (one every ten minutes). Despite this, the creation of newly generated Bitcoins will decrease geometrically over time, meaning a fifty percent reduction every four years. This means that the maximum number of Bitcoins in existence (twenty-one million) will not be reached for quite some time (2140, according to bitcoin.org).

Bitcoins can either be mined or someone can buy, trade, or exchange goods and/or services for the currency. A miner receives Bitcoins for "free" (except for electricity) by solving difficult blocks of mathematical equations (bitcoin.com). One miner competes against other miners to finish the block of equations first; the first one to finish receives the reward (Bitcoins). Anyone can mine Bitcoins as long as they have a basic knowledge of computers and understand the fundamental principles of how the Bitcoin software works.

In order to mine, a person needs a computer that has an internet connection at all times with an operating system such as Windows, Ubuntu, or Linux and a special type of graphics card, Advance Micro Device (AMD). The miner will also need the CGMiner program or GUIMiner is also reputable (bitcoinmining.com). These mining programs do three things: one, they keep your system running (controls temperatures, fan speeds, temperature cutoffs, and temperature targets; basically anything that your graphic card controls) second, they keep a connection between your computer and the system that is giving the block of mathematical equations, and the third thing is that they keep track of your blocks of solved equations and the rewards that one receives. Each miner sets up a username (worker name) and a worker ID (password) within one of these mining programs.

It is easier to mine in pools, which basically consist of other miners who "pool" (I described this type of teamwork earlier as peer-to-peer) their computer power in order to solve the blocks of equations quicker. If you join a pool, the equations you are given to solve will be smaller and easier while the combined efforts of the other miners means that the blocks are solved quicker, which means you can earn more Bitcoins. It also means that the rewards earned have to be split among the other members of the pool, but this will ultimately be worth it, because miners will be consistent in solving the blocks meaning one is more likely to receive a good reward.

You may be wondering what someone can do with Bitcoins once they obtain the elusive currency. Owners of Bitcoins can hold on to them, or they can trade them in to online exchanges, who will exchange them for other currencies. "Owners of Bitcoin can use various websites to trade them for physical currencies, such as United States dollars or Euros, or can exchange them for goods and services from a number of vendors" (Britannica

Educational Publishing, 2013). "Bitcoins are used to order goods online, for real world services, and, for those so inclined, illegal drugs and weapons from the Internet's underbelly" (Mont, 2013).

In order to begin mining, a miner must download a digital wallet and create an account (bitcoinmining.com). "Bitcoin accounts are listed simply as a string of letters and numbers with no names attached, giving a level of anonymity impossible with debit and credit cards or even PayPal accounts" (Westwood, 2013). This digital wallet allows a miner to make electronic transactions. Digital wallets keep a miner's Bitcoins more secure, it would be too risky for a miner to store his Bitcoins on his hard drive. By mining Bitcoins, a person puts a lot of stress on his computer, so, if they store their Bitcoins on the hard drive and the computer happens to crash, they have lost all of their Bitcoins and their hard work was for nothing. Digital wallets also keep Bitcoins safer from potential hackers.

Some of the most attractive features of Bitcoin are, one, the anonymity the currency can provide and, two, Bitcoin is independent of any banking authority. Block chain helps to keep the currency anonymous, but only to a certain degree. Block chain keeps track of all transactions made, but the record is made only of the receiver's addresses; however, individual's names remain a secret. The addresses are like privately run bank accounts, only keeping track of transactions made and stipulate that if the data is lost, so are all the Bitcoins mined or stored. "Bitcoin, in other words, survives because of what you can see and what you cannot. Users are hidden, but transactions are exposed. The code is visible to all, but its origins are mysterious. The currency is both real and elusive--just like its founder" (Davis, 2011).

There are speculators out there that believe Bitcoin is a type of Ponzi scheme, but that is not the case because the Bitcoin system does not promise a high reward to any one person. Bitcoin is decentralized and there is not one person who has control of the currency, meaning the system cannot be undermined and the funds disappear. Bitcoin does not have a type of intermediation, which means the users can buy or sell the currency without interference. There are not more benefits for one user and not another, except for maybe those who benefit from an increase in exchange rates (which would happen with any type of currency) or those who dedicate more time and computing power to mining and, in turn, receive more rewards (Bitcoins.)

The fact that Bitcoin is independent of any banking authority means that there is not a government behind it interfering with it causing inflation and the banking industry cannot control it either; the value of a Bitcoin is determined through its desirability. "Gavin Andersen, Bitcoin Foundation's chief scientist, says Bitcoin still remains an experiment." Bitcoin may still be considered an experiment, but the possibilities of this experiment are extremely stimulating.

HOW TO GET YOUR VIRTUAL HANDS ON BITCOIN?

Get free Bitcoin from Bitcoin Faucets

A Bitcoin faucet is a website that gives you free fractions of Bitcoin just for visiting. They make income with ads and they pay visitors fractions of Bitcoin called Satoshis, which is also the name of inventor of Bitcoin algorithm. You can withdraw at any time once you have the minimum amount to do a withdrawal.

Visit each of these websites and claim Bitcoins. You can claim many times every day.

One of the most popular bitcoin faucets, moonbitcoin. It is one of the most reputable, highest traffic, bitcoin faucets on the internet. The massive traffic allows advertisers to make greater payments for ad space, enabling visitors with freer bitcoin and guaranteed pay-outs.

Make Bitcoin with Your Computer & Graphic Card

You can make free Bitcoin with your computer power. This method is now easy, thanks to the new software which allow users easily setup and begin mining with their computers without having trouble to configure programmatically the scripts. You must sign up for one of those websites, install their app and let it run when you want to make bitcoin.

NiceHash is a special multi-mining pool MinerGate is a mining pool created by as it allows users to mine any hashing a group of crypto coin enthusiasts, algorithm and to sell the hashing. It is the first pool with merged mining. Algorithm in the Nicehash hashpower This means that while mining you can exchange to users that want to buy a mine different coins simultaneously profitable mining contract. without decrease of hash rate.

Make Bitcoin with Cloud Mining Providers

Cloud Mining is a way to mine bitcoin (or different cryptocurrencies) without the need of owning a miner (or mining hardware). Simply said, you buy yourself some shares of mining power – like a mining pool – and profit together with the pool. This means that you only need a contract with someone who offers Cloud Mining Services and a bitcoin wallet.

Cloud Mining services are for you if you want to invest in bitcoin mining without the hassle of managing your own hardware, or, in some cases can't invest in high priced ASIC mining hardware. You can use the cloud mining to earn your coins.

Genesis-Mining is the world's leading and most transparent hosted hashpower provider for Bitcoin and Altcoins. Reliable & Customer Oriented.

Reinvest to multiply

This is so obvious, if you want to get bigger piece of cake, just invest some pennies. Your investment soldiers working for you. If Every-time you make some small amounts of BTC and you don't really need Just to invest it, you'll get it back later with some profits.

The sweetest part is when you leverage your investments with referrals bonuses. In a few months you gold mine is working for you on autopilot. Isn't that sweet.

Bitcoin Wallets

The software that helps a user manage his/ her funds is called a wallet. The functions of the wallet software are to hold (securely) the user's private keys, create transactions that are sent to the network, and collect incoming and outgoing transactions to show the balance of available funds to the user. As a user can own many addresses, most software wallets are ready to manage multiple addresses, aggregating the funds across them.

All wallet software can create new addresses, for instance when it is run for the very first time. To create a new address a key generation algorithm is executed.

Creating a Bitcoin address is straightforward and instantaneous. There are many kinds of Bitcoin wallets:

Online bitcoin wallets

Web-based wallets store your private keys online. Several such online services are available, and some of them link to mobile and desktop wallets, replicating your addresses between different devices that you own.

- Coinbase
- Blockchain

Desktop wallets

If you have installed the original bitcoin client (Bitcoin Core), then you are running a wallet, but may not even know it. In addition to relaying transactions on the network, this software also enables you to create a bitcoin address for sending and receiving the virtual currency, and to store the private key for it.

- Bitcoin.org
- Electrum
- Mobile wallets

Desktop-based wallets are all very well, but they aren't very useful if you are out on the street, trying to pay for something in a physical store.

This is where a mobile wallet comes in handy. Running as an app on your smartphone, the wallet can store the private keys for your bitcoin addresses, and enable you to pay for things directly with your phone.

Ledger USB wallet

Ledger Wallet protects your keys with a secure micro-processor certified against all types of attacks (both physical and logical). This technology has been used in the banking industry for decades (think credit card chips). Our hardware wallet will do all the Bitcoin cryptographic heavy lifting such as signing transactions inside its secure environment. You can therefore use your Bitcoins with maximum trust, even on an insecure or compromised computer.

Paper wallets

A paper wallet is a document that contains copies of the public and private keys that make up a wallet. Often it will have QR codes, so that you can quickly scan them and add the keys into a software wallet to make a transaction.

What is Blockchain?

As a new user, you can get started with Bitcoin without understanding the technical details. Once you have installed a Bitcoin wallet on your computer or mobile phone, it will generate your first Bitcoin address and you can create more whenever you need one. You can disclose your addresses to your friends so that they can pay you or vice versa. In fact, this is pretty similar to how email works, except that Bitcoin addresses should only be used once.

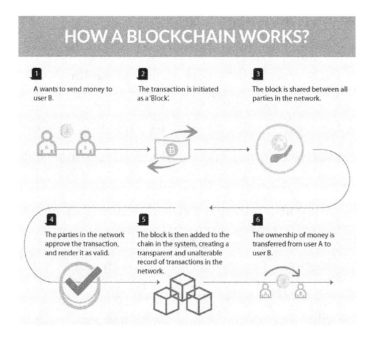

Balances - block chain

The block chain is a shared public ledger on which the entire Bitcoin network relies. All confirmed transactions are included in the block chain. This way, Bitcoin wallets can calculate their spendable balance and new transactions can be verified to be spending bitcoins that are actually owned by the spender. The integrity and the chronological order of the block chain are enforced with cryptography.

Transactions - private keys

A transaction is a transfer of value between Bitcoin wallets that gets included in the block chain. Bitcoin wallets keep a secret piece of data called a private key or seed, which is used to sign transactions, providing a mathematical proof that they have come from the owner of the wallet. The signature also prevents the transaction from being altered by anybody once it has been issued. All transactions are broadcast between users and usually begin to be confirmed by the network in the following 10 minutes, through a process called mining.

Mining

Mining is a distributed consensus system that is used to confirm waiting transactions by including them in the block chain. It enforces a chronological order in the block chain, protects the neutrality of the network, and allows different computers to agree on the state of the system. To be confirmed, transactions must be packed in a block that fits very strict cryptographic rules that will be verified by the network. These rules prevent previous blocks from being modified because doing so would invalidate all following blocks. Mining also creates the equivalent of a competitive lottery that prevents any individual from easily adding new blocks consecutively in the block chain. This way, no individual can control what is included in the block chain or replace parts of the block chain to roll back their own spends.

Get First Blockchain Account

Open Bitcoin Account

Step 1:

Go to website- https://blockchain.info/wallet/#/

Step 2:

Click – Create new Blockchain Wallet and Fill the details (Remember email and passwords)

Step 3:

Get Started

Step 4:

Click –Start Receiving Bitcoins

Step 5:

1. Copy the Bitcoin Address like this-
1PnSjJtAaAEe4gpA6aenA6hQAvDt4ckRnX This
Bitcoin Address like the bank account number. So
don't forget it.

2. Check your email and Click Conformation link

Step 5:

1. Click OK

2. It will show your wallet id and ask for password

3. It is important to note down this wallet id
(d2c2ycfc-9fee-4dc0-bdcf-61e6d6d29e7d). This is
like your name on the bank account

4. Enter password and Click signin

5. Top it will shows some popup. Need again verify
your email account

Step 6:

Check your email account and Click verificatuion
link

Secure Account

Step 1:

Click Security Center on the left side of the page

Step 2:

1. Click mobile verification and your mobile
number

2. Get one time password on mobile and enter it on the web page

Step 3:

1. Click two step verification

2. Again received one time password and enter it

Step 4:

Click Settings and you can see Auto logout timing on downside, can change it

Transfer Bitcoins

1. Click Transaction

2. Enter your bitcoin address on From address

3. Enter opponent bitcoin address at To field

4. Enter amount of BTC and click next step

5. Transaction fee for every transaction is 0.0001 BTC

COIN BASE

What is Coin Base?

Coinbase is a secure online bitcoin exchange for buying, selling, sending, receiving, and storing bitcoin. Coinbase is different from other bitcoin services in several ways.

Nothing comes close to Coinbase in terms of ease of use and security. You link a bank account to the San Francisco-based start-up, and then send them money to buy Bitcoin at the currently offered price. They wait up to a few days to ensure your transaction clears (Bitcoin is a murky financial area, and they don't want to risk identity theft or other problems until they have banks on their side), and then give you access to your coins. 30 days after you have a successful transaction, you can add a credit card to your account to enable "instant buys" of up to $1,000 per week. Regular speed buys are allowed at up to $50,000 per week, from a linked bank account. Their platform is very popular, and justifiably so—it makes owning and managing your coins very simple. They also take excellent   security   precautions—two-factor authentication on log-in AND on send, keeping the VAST majority (97%!) of their coins in offline storage, and so on. They are an excellent way to enter the Bitcoin ecosystem, and an excellent way to integrate Bitcoin into your business, if you're so inclined. They also offer the excellent Coinbase Vault program–a system that allows you to place your coins into a very high-security lock, requiring two-factor authentication along with a mandatory waiting period before the coins can be moved.

What aren't they? They are not an exchange. They aren't a trading platform. If your goal is to be buying and selling Bitcoin on its swings, you don't want to be using Coinbase for your day-to-day trading.

Details:

1. Backed by Andreessen Horowitz

2. Biggest US player, focused on merchant integration

3. Easy platform for buying and selling

4. Good way to get money into the ecosystem

5. High fees and long waits make it unsuited for trading. It's more like Western Union than like Scottrade.

Pros:

1. Easy to use! No harder than PayPal

2. Secure, trustworthy, American

3. Good customer service

4. They pay your transaction fees when you move your Bitcoin around

Cons:

1. Fees of about 1%

2. Long lag time for initial purchase, and later purchases over 1BTC makes it hard to profit from market movement over the short term

3. Slightly higher than market price for purchase

4. Really just not intended to be used for trading

5. Will occasionally cancel orders for "high-risk behavior

A 1% fee for each transfer from bitcoin to your local currency ($, €, £) or from your local currency to bitcoin. User is responsible for miner's fee on external transactions less than 0.0003 BTC. Sending between Coinbase users is always free.

Minimum fee of $0.15. Incoming wire fee is $10. Wire withdrawal fee is $25. For Canadian users, there is a $1 fee on all CAD deposits and withdrawals. A 3% convenience charge is assessed on purchases using credit and debit cards.

Coin base Account

If you sign up for the Coinbase program and refer someone you both get $1 worth of free BTC when they sign up for a Coinbase wallet account bitcoin qt import wallet. To store your Bitcoins you need a wallet such as this service so this is a great starting point to have in case you need this digital safe. Coinbase is an international digital wallet that allows you to securely buy, use, and accept the Bitcoin currency (BTC).

Step 1: Sign up via this Coinbase Link to get $1 worth of free Bitcoin. You will need to add a phone and verify your bank account.

Step 2: Connect your bank account with Coinbase to start buying and selling Bitcoin.

Step 3: Referral Bonus is paid. The referral bonuses are only paid if the new user verifies the new Coinbase account by adding a phone and verifying a bank account from one of their supported countries. The $1 BTC payout will usually arrive within 10 minutes of completing the account, but it may take longer.

Get First Bitcoin to Wallet

1. Go to https://freebitco.in/

2. Signup using email id and bitcoin address

3. Click claim bitcoin

4. Click I am not robot. .Select correct pictures (to show you are not robot) and click verify

5. Click Roll and Get Random Number

6. Payout based on below table. There is a chance to win Highest 0.45125336 BTC (Around 200 Dollars) and Lowest 0.00000199 (0.003 Dollars). But it is highly random and lower chance to high payout.

7. Have to withdraw Freebitco Bitcoin to your Blackchain Wallet. Click Lottery and Click Withdraw.

Manual Withdraw:

The minimum amount that you can withdraw is 0.00010400 BTC.

After you initiate a withdrawal request, the Bitcoins will be sent to your wallet within 6 hours and you will be able to see the withdrawal transaction by clicking on STATS in the top menu and then on PERSONAL STATS in the STATS page.

0.00000400 BTC will be deducted from the withdrawal amount to pay the transaction fee. If you make additional withdrawal requests while you have one pending, the amounts will be clubbed together and you will only pay the transaction fee once.

Automatic Withdraw:

If you want auto withdraw, Tick auto withdraw. If you enable auto withdraw and your balance is more than 0.00025000 BTC, it will be sent out as a payment to your Bitcoin wallet on Sunday.

BITCOIN MINING

Where do bitcoins come from? With paper money, a government decides when to print and distribute money. Bitcoin doesn't have a central government.

With Bitcoin, miners use special software to solve math problems and are issued a certain number of bitcoins in exchange. This provides a smart way to issue the currency and also creates an incentive for more people to mine.

Bitcoin miners help keep the Bitcoin network secure by approving transactions. Mining is an important and integral part of Bitcoin that ensures fairness while keeping the Bitcoin network stable, safe and secure.

While the actual process of Bitcoin mining is handled by the Bitcoin mining hardware itself, special Bitcoin mining software is needed to connect your Bitcoin miners to the blockchain and your Bitcoin mining pool as well, if you are part of a Bitcoin mining pool.

The software delivers the work to the miners and receives the completed work from the miners and relays that information back to the blockchain and your mining pool. The best Bitcoin mining software can run on almost any operating system, such as OSX, Windows, Linux, and has even been ported to work on a Raspberry Pi with some modifications for drivers depending on your mining setup.

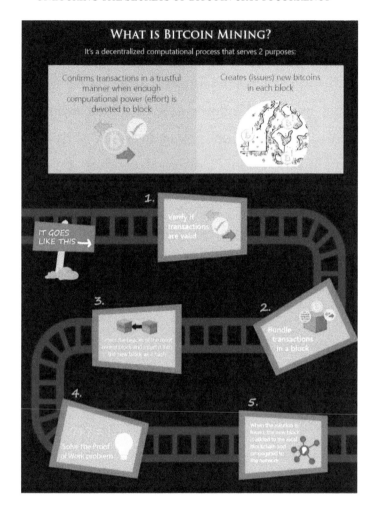

(Image Source: BitcoinMining.com).

Not only does the Bitcoin mining software relay the input and output of your Bitcoin miners to the blockchain, but it also monitors them and displays general statistics such as the temperature, hashrate, fan speed, and average speed of the Bitcoin miner.

There are a few different types of Bitcoin mining software out there and each have their own advantages and disadvantages.

Try First Mining using windows or OSX:

A very good mining software is BitMinter. It is, by far, the easiest to use. It comes with its own software, making things so much easier. Below are the few parts that involve the creation and setup of your account.

1) Open up a web browser and navigate to the BitMinter log in (https://bitminter.com/login).

2) Choose your account you'd like to link with BitMinter. Log in with this account. BitMinter uses a log in service called OpenID, which is a futuristic way of logging in with an already-existing account to eliminate the need to remember yet another password.

3) Set the main settings as according to the picture:

- Set your email address.

- Set your auto cash out threshold to a reasonable amount. Mine is set to 1 BTC (approx. $10). This means that when I mine 1 BTC, I will receive it into my bitcoin wallet, just like the test, but with a higher number of bitcoins.

- Set your "Pay to address" to the address that we used in the Step 3 to test the wallet. This is the address that all of your bitcoins are sent to, in case you haven't figured that out yet.

Each computer needs its own worker to connect to on the BitMinter server. The software (in the next step) on each computer will each be set up to a different worker so that the BitMinter server doesn't have trouble transmitting and receiving mining work.

While still logged into the BitMinter website, hover over "My Account" at the top of the page. Then click on "Workers".

Near the bottom of the page, there are two fields under the "Name" and "Password" headers. Give your new worker a name like "Laptop", or "New Dell". Create a short password. Remember the password for the worker. Then click "Add".

Click "Home" in the navigation bar at the top of the page.

Most people already have Java installed, but if you don't, follow this step.

1) Go to www.java.com/download.

2) Click "Free Java Download".

3) Click "Agree and Start Free Download".

4) Depending on your operating system, a different version of the file will download.

5) Follow the onscreen instructions to continue installing the software.

6) Click finish and be done installing. Continue on to the next step to set up a miner.

Go back to the BitMinter homepage. Click on the "Engine Start" button. This will download a Java Web Starter, which will download the actual program and install it.

Use this file to start the program in the future. When it starts, you will see a program that looks like the first picture.

Set up the software by linking it to your worker created in Step 7. "Click Settings" > "Account...". Beside "User Name:" use the username you created when creating the BitMinter account. Beside "Worker Name:" and "Worker Password:" enter the worker name and worker password you created in Step 6.

If the window is small, click the button in the bottom right corner of the screen. Then click the "Engine Start" button beside each of the devices you want to use. For reference, Test all of your devices, but you should really only bother running devices that get you 25 Mhps or above.

Go to Settings > Options to change these settings. Look at the fourth picture to set it up like how I have it set up. The picture has expainations.

Automated devices are a list of devices that you set so that you can start them on their own automatically when the software starts

BITCOIN MINING AND MINING DIFFICULTY

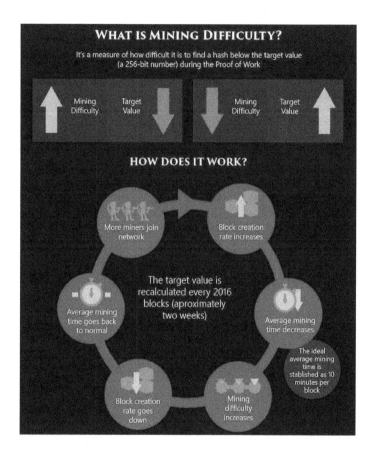

Choosing the Right Wallet

Now let's choose our wallet. Choosing the right wallet depends on several factors. Keep in mind that it's pretty easy to switch between wallets, so it's not a life or death question. Here are the factors I would take into account when choosing my wallet:

Frequency of use

How often are you planning on sending out Bitcoins? Notice that I ask only about sending Bitcoins since receiving Bitcoins is pretty much the same for all types of wallets.

If you think you're going to be a heavy Bitcoin user I suggest using a wallet that is easily accessible on your mobile phone so that it will always be available.

However, if you're just buying Bitcoins for a long term investment I suggest finding an independent wallet so you know your Bitcoins are in your hands alone.

How many Bitcoins you plan on owning

If you're just going to buy a small amount of Bitcoins then it doesn't really matter which wallet you use since the risk isn't that big. If however you are planning to spend a considerable amount of money on your newly purchased Bitcoins you may want to consider using a multisig wallet or even an independent hardware wallet which are considered to be safer in general.

User-friendliness

How easy is it to access the wallet, send Bitcoins and receive funds? Some wallets have a great user interface while others tend to lag behind with an interface that will scare any new Bitcoiner away.

Personal paranoia and anonymity preferences

How paranoid are you about someone stealing your Bitcoins? This of course varies from one person to the other, but many people in the Bitcoin ecosystem don't trust anyone but themselves. Also, certain 3rd party wallets require that you sign up with your name and email you give away your anonymity by choosing this wallet. Here are my top picks depending on the various factors I've just covered:

Coinbase

3rd party wallet. Very user friendly, easy to set up and you also get a $5 bonus when signing up. Coinbase offers a mobile and a web interface for their wallet. The company is very reputable in the Bitcoin space. Using this wallet is great if you're a newbie who isn't planning on storing a lot of money in his wallet and don't care that much about staying anonymous.

Blockchain.info

3rd party wallet. A semi user-friendly wallet which has a mobile and web interface. It's a bit harder to get around than Coinbase but it's much more secure as the company doesn't have direct access to your Bitcoins. Anonymity is still compromised but at least you have more control over your coins.

TREZOR

Independent wallet. If you're planning on holding large amounts of money you should use TREZOR. This is a hardware wallet which is almost as secure as you can get with your coins. Anonymity is completely maintained, the only issue is that since it's an actual product it will cost you money. However, considering the fact that it protects your investment, it may be worth it. I would go with TREZOR if I needed to store a large amount of coins which I will rarely spend.

GREENADDRESS

Independent wallet. Green address is a semi user-friendly multisig wallet that has a mobile and web version. Security and privacy are completely maintained and it has become a very favorable wallet throughout the Bitcoin community. This is a great alternative for using Blockchain.info.

You can also choose to distribute your coins between several wallets, this way if something goes wrong you don't have all of your eggs in one basket. But if you're reading this guide my guess is that you're new to Bitcoin and aren't planning on buying a large amount of coins to begin with. If that is indeed the case, any of the wallets mentioned above will do the job nicely.

Go ahead and choose your wallet - install its app on your mobile phone or create an account through the relevant website.

EAU-COIN

Independent wallet. EAU-COIN is a blockchain based currency. In case you don't understand what that means, there is no one bank, one person, or one country that owns or holds EAU-COIN.

When an investor buys EAU-COIN, that person become part of the blockchain of EAU-COIN, and their coins are a real part of the bank itself that they co-own with everyone else.

Blockchain ledger information from the moment of cryptocurrency coin issue, is shared worldwide between all EAU-COIN owners. Every investor can check if any one particular owner has the EAU-COINs that they say they do. So, when it comes to using EAU-COIN for any transaction such as buying a coffee, lunch or a new home, everything is secure and certain.

EAU-COIN's blockchain is so widely spread, that any catastrophe affecting any one or even several georgraphic locations, has no effect on the overall accountability of its performance, at any time. Information will be restored immediately any catastrophe passes, from the unaffected blockchain to those areas affected, and the entire blcokchan will continue as if nothing had happened.

This built-in systemic security cannot be said of central banks, their subject banks, or networks, who by profile, are legally obliged to backup and store their information daily in only three separate locations. EAU-COIN is therefore, far more secure than traditional banking- and I draw the reader's attention to only two current examples of catastrophe, such as the two month long failure of TSB, UK's systems, and the recent Visa card down debarcle that affected the whole of Europe, and took 4 days or more, to bring back online, bit by bit.

Bitcoin – The Advantages

With an understanding of Bitcoins and how they work, we will discuss the advantages to using Bitcoins.

Virtual currency is more efficient than hard cash. According to Plassaras (2013), scholars state that digital money can perform functions of currency more efficiently than traditional fiat currencies (government-backed). There are three functions a currency serves: first, it acts as a medium of exchange; second, it acts as a unit of account and expresses a certain purchasing power; and third, it acts as a store of value for future spending. Bitcoin has the potential to perform these roles more efficiently than physical money.

Reasons to use Bitcoin have been described by supports of digital currencies: first, it has an anonymous peer-to-peer payment system; second, to avoid reliance on a third party such as a government central bank or any commercial bank; third, cryptography replaces trust; fourth, to avoid inflation or collapse of a currency altogether; and fifth, to circumvent transaction costs incurred by credit card companies and bank fees.

The Disadvantages

After having understood the advantages of the use of Bitcoins, we will have a look at the disadvantages that are recognized in literature. Naturally, there are negative aspects when using a virtual currency. As we will see, Bitcoins can be considered a bad alternative to traditional money, because virtual currencies promote criminal activity such as: money laundering, drug trafficking, double payments, computer hacking and terrorism. However, none of these activities is endemic to the use of Bitcoins.

There are other negative aspects to using a virtual currency that do not have to do with criminality such as speculative investment, unpredictability, and irreplaceability of Bitcoins. Finally, there is a lack of places to use or spend Bitcoins. Bitcoin users bear all the risks.

CHAPTER THREE

PURCHASE YOUR COINS

Trading Bitcoins with PayPal
Buy Bitcoins with PayPal Through Virwox

Since no exchange currently allows a way around the charge back issues of buying Bitcoins with PayPal we are going to have to go through VirWox – The Virtual World Exchange. We will use a virtual currency called SLL (Second Life Linden Dollars). This currency is used for one of the biggest virtual worlds today – Second Life. After buying this currency with PayPal (which is acceptable) we will then trade it to Bitcoins.

My guess is that Virwox is able to do this method since they are not directly selling you Bitcoins with PayPal but rather selling you SLL with PayPal which they can prove if you received (unlike Bitcoin since it's anonymous in nature).

Things you should know about Virwox before we get started:

Because of chargeback risk Virwox is taking on, they are limiting the amount you can deposit initially through PayPal or a credit card. Here are the exact limits according to their website from April 30th 2015.

This process holds within it more transaction fees than usual. This may still be a valid solution since the soaring numbers of BTC compensate for this. It's important for you to be aware of the different transaction fees.

VirWox is delaying new user transactions for up to 48 hours. This means that it can take you 2 days to complete this process (still way faster than using a wire transfer).

If you still don't receive the Bitcoins after 48 hours (which is very unusual) you can contact Virwox at support@virwox.com.

If you find yourself getting stuck at any point don't hesitate to contact me through the contact form on the site.

Step 1: Go to VirWox.

VirWox is an exchange of virtual currency. You can buy Lindens, Bitcoins, and more. It has more than 400,000 registered users and is a Second Life Lindens authorized reseller.

Step 2: Open a free account

Click on the "Not registered yet" on the top of the left sidebar to open up a new account as shown here:

Step 3: Fill out our personal details

Fill out your username and email address. Where it asks for "avatar name" just leave it at "No Avatar", it doesn't matter, since you're not going to play Second Life.

Continue filling out all of the personal details and click "register".

Step 4: Activate your account

Once you clicked "register" you will get an email confirmation with your password. Open the email, copy the password and log back into VirWox.

Step 5: IMPORTANT!!! Change your password!

After clicking the confirmation link it is advised you change your password as shown below since you will be transferring money through this site.

Do not worry about the message saying "Your avatar connection has not been validated yet" – it is irrelevant.

Step 6: Fund your account through PayPal

Click on deposit on the left side and choose PayPal Express. Fund the account with how many USD you'd like.

Note: From now on, for each transaction you will make there will be a fee – make sure you are aware of the relevant deposit and withdrawal fees.

Step 7: Buy SLL with USD

Go to Exchange->USD/SLL on the left side. You can also go to any other currency you'd like. Buy SLL (which mean Second Life Lindens). We will later on exchange these SLL to Bitcoins.

Note: If you haven't made a deposit yet you will get the screen shown above requesting you to deposit before you buy SLL.

Step 8: Buy BTC with SLL

Once you have SLL in your account, go to the BTC/SLL and buy Bitcoins with your SLL.

Important!!!

Sometimes a manual review will be required by VirWox after this step. This can take up to 48 hours but usually takes around 6 hours.

Step 9: Withdraw your Bitcoins

Choose "Withdraw" on the left side and send the Bitcoins to your wallet.

How many fees will be deducted from my deposit?

This is probably the second most asked question I get. It's important to understand that when you buy Bitcoins through Virwox you are actually conducting two transactions. USD to SLL and SLL to BTC. This means you'll need to pay a fee for each of these transactions.

The problem is that Virwox's fee structure is always changing. That is why I advise to check each case in person before proceeding. There is a pretty cool site which shows you the current BTC/USD rate after all of Virwox's fees. I'm not sure how reliable the site is but you can check it out for yourself here.

Buy Bitcoins with PayPal through Circle (US only)

It turns out there's a really simple hack you can do to get Bitcoins with PayPal instantly using Circle. There are a few limitations though:

1. You need to live in the US

2. You need to have a verified PayPal account linked to a credit card/bank account

If you're OK with these two limitations then you're good to go. Here's how it's done.

Step 1 – Open a Circle account

Head up to Circle and open an account. I've reviewed Circle before and it's a great service provider for buying Bitcoins with a credit card. Opening an account is pretty straight-forward and you shouldn't run into any problems.

Step 2 – Get a PayPal Debit MasterCard

If you already have a PayPal Debit MasterCard (not to confuse with a PayPal prepaid card) then you can skip this step. If not, you can apply here. Application takes a few minutes, and includes the result if you're approved or denied. Once approved, it can take between 2 to 4 weeks to receive your card in the mail. Once the card arrives you'll need to activate it by calling a toll free number or through logging into your account.

Step 3 – Connect your PayPal Debit MasterCard to your Circle account

Go to your account -> settings -> linked accounts and click on "add account". You can then enter the details of your PayPal debit MasterCard.

Step 4 – Buy Bitcoins with PayPal instantly!

Once your card is connected you can now buy Bitcoins and your PayPal balance will be the first to be used in this purchase. You can also sell Bitcoins and withdraw the dollar balance back to your card.

Buy Bitcoins with PayPal through Local Bitcoins

If both options above haven't worked for you (and at least one of them should), you can try buying Bitcoins with PayPal through Local Bitcoins.

How to buy Bitcoins using Local Bitcoins

Local Bitcoins, unlike Virwox is a marketplace where buyers and sellers meet. If you use this option you'll be dealing with an actual person which means that credibility also comes into play. The way you can use Local Bitcoins to buy Bitcoins with PayPal is by finding a person that is willing to sell them to you.

But since the seller is taking a big risk (as I explained in the beginning of this post) they will usually charge a really big premium (most of the times this will be more expensive than Virwox). The upside is that you will usually get your Bitcoins faster.

Step 1: Enter your search parameters

The first step will be to go to Local Bitcoins and enter how much you want to buy and from which country. Since Local Bitcoins was originally made for people to meet face to face there is no "worldwide" search which is a shame. This means that there is no way to see all of the people who are willing to sell you with PayPal worldwide other than going through each country one at a time.

Step 2: Choose your seller

On the next screen you'll see a list of available sellers; you can now browse them one by one.

Here are the things to take into account:

Feedback score – Located under the seller's name. It's advised to conduct transactions only with high feedback sellers.

Trade limits – Each seller has a minimum/maximum amount of Bitcoins he's willing to trade

Payment window – How much time you have for paying the purchase and marking the payment done after you initiate a trade.

It's also super important to read the terms of trade for the specific seller located on the right side.

Some sellers will require you have an initial reputation in order to buy from them so they can avoid scams or fraud. This means that you will perhaps have to conduct some small transactions just to get reputation.

Step 3: Complete the trade

Once you've found your seller just enter how much you want to buy and click on "Send trade request". Keep in mind that it's crucial to conduct all communications within Local Bitcoins and preferably use their Escrow services (which are triggered automatically for all online sales).

How To Buy Bitcoins Using Coinbase

Coinbase has a pretty intuitive website which makes it pretty easy to buy Bitcoins from. Start off by signing up to Coinbase. After signing up go to "payment methods" and choose "add a bank account". Coinbase currently supports 25 countries.

After you've entered your bank account you'll be asked to verify your account. You can do this is one of two ways:

1. Get billed for 2 small amounts (up to $1). After you see these amounts in your bank statement you can just fill them in and get verified. This takes

about 2 days and can be somewhat annoying, but it's much safer than the other option.

2. Supply Coinbase with your customer number and access code so they can verify you own this bank account. Keep in mind that your access code IS NOT YOUR PIN. If you don't know how to get your access code just Google your bank's name and "access code" and you'll probably see how in a second.

After you verify your bank account you will need to verify your phone number as well. Once you finish your account verification just go to "Buy Bitcoin", enter the amount you wish to buy and click the "Buy Bitcoin" button at the bottom.

Keep in mind that a verified account at Coinbase has a limit of $3,000 worth of Bitcoins per day.

How To Buy Bitcoins Using Circle (International credit card needed)

Circle is one of the hottest new startups at the moment which allow you to buy Bitcoins with a credit card pretty easily. The company just came out of Beta, and they claim to operate in the US.

However numerous users (including myself) have managed to purchase Bitcoins through them using an international credit card even though they do not reside in the US.

First sign up for Circle:

After you finish the signup process go to "Add funds" and deposit money into your account using your credit card.

If you didn't add a credit card on sign-up, you will be asked to do so during this step.

You should see the money in your account instantly. Once the money is in the account, you can withdraw it to your own Bitcoin wallet in the form of BTC. Go to "Send money" -> click on the "USD" sign and it will convert into BTC. Then just fill out your Bitcoin address and the amount you want to withdraw.

How to buy Bitcoins using CoinMama (No verification needed up to $500, worldwide)

CoinMama specializes in Bitcoin purchases through a credit card. They take a premium fee for their services but they do not limit you to a maximum amount of Bitcoins that you can buy. You can buy up to $500 worth of Bitcoin without verification. Another good feature CoinMama offers is that once you place your order with them your price is reserved. So if the Bitcoin price goes up while you are purchasing, your price remains the same until you finish the payment process and you will be unaffected.

From Coinmama's homepage you can choose how many Bitcoins you'd like to buy/sell. You can enter the price either in BTC or in USD or choose one of the offered packages.

Once finished, click "Buy Bitcoins" and you will be taken to the sign-up page. After you fill out your initial details you will need to go through additional verification by submitting a photo ID document. Verification is usually pretty quick (it took me 1.5 hours to get verified). You can also buy up to $500 without doing the verification process. Once verified you can buy Bitcoins pretty easily with your credit card through the simple interface. If you verified your address I suggest you use

"Visa, MasterCard via Simplex" since it's the fastest option. If you want to continue without verification you can use the "MoneyGram" option. You can then pay the amount with your credit card on MoneyGram's website (this is applicable to US residents only).

The next step will be to enter your own Bitcoin address. Unlike other exchanges, CoinMama doesn't keep your Bitcoins on their wallet (which is a good thing). This means you'll need to get a Bitcoin wallet before continuing.

The last step will be to enter your payment details and place your order.

Coinmama uses the services of Simplex, allowing merchants to sell Bitcoins via credit cards as a payment method. I'll probably be doing a more in-depth review of Coinmama soon, as it has become quite a popular method for buying Bitcoins.

How to buy Bitcoins using Coin.MX (Verification needed, worldwide, $5 bonus on first deposit)

Coin.MX is a marketplace for Bitcoins. Prices are around 1.3% higher than what you would find in Coinbase and you will also have to go through a user verification process in order to deposit money. All in all this is probably the simplest solution for buying with a credit card. If you're a first time customer at Coin.MX you'll get a $5 deposit bonus in your account.

User verification takes around 48 hours and requires uploading a short video of you holding a readable government issued document (e.g. passport). Once you've been verified, depositing funds is pretty simple and easy – just go to "deposit" and add your credit card details and you're able to buy Bitcoins.

Withdrawing your Bitcoins is pretty easy as well – keep in mind that there's a 0.001BTC withdrawal fee required. Just go to "Deposit", select "BTC" and paste your Bitcoin address.

5 Golden Rules when Buying Bitcoins

Rule #1 – Check the credibility of your Bitcoin seller

When buying from an individual, validate their reputation by reviewing their trader profile if one is available. Ask for a Facebook, LinkedIn or any other social network profile in order to ascertain there's an actual person behind the screen. As a rule of thumb, never buy Bitcoins from someone who you cannot account for their credibility.

If you're buying at an exchange, check for the exchange name and the word "reviews". Looking for reviews about exchanges and even individuals in the Bitcointalk forum can also provide valuable insights.

Rule #2 – Document everything

Since Bitcoin is somewhat untraceable like cash, in case of fraud it will be hard to prove specific allegations. Make sure you document your communication with the seller in a way that will be easy to present if needed later on.

Rule #3 – when dealing with individuals: Wait for confirmation before paying

For small to medium transaction it's recommended to wait for at least one confirmation before submitting your payment. For larger transactions, wait at least 6 confirmations.

Rule #4 – Use escrow when needed

When conducting large transactions with individuals, use a Bitcoin escrow service to hold on to your funds until you receive the required amount of confirmations. This way your money will be in the custody of a trusted 3rd party until you receive the Bitcoins.

Rule #5 – NEVER leave your money at an exchange

If you're buying Bitcoins at an exchange, make sure to move your Bitcoins to your own private Bitcoin wallet the moment you get them. NEVER leave Bitcoins inside an exchange; this can result in the loss of your Bitcoins due to theft or fraud.

CHAPTER FOUR

BITCOIN: BEYOND MONEY

BITCOIN is more than a new currency. Bitcoin and other virtual currencies are creating a new architecture for exchanging information over the Internet that is peer to peer, open yet secure, and nearly frictionless. Imagine how other systems that rely on intermediaries, such as property transfer, contract execution, and identity management, could be disrupted by a similarly open peer-to-peer system.

System of payment

Bitcoin reduces friction in payments. Currently, when an individual transfers funds, he or she must work with a third party. This intermediary, such as a credit card or payments company, often exacts high fees. For example, for remittances, there is an average fee of 9 percent, with some banks charging an additional fee of up to 5 percent for turning the remittance into cash.7

Bitcoin allows for a direct payment to any-one, anywhere in the world, at any time. With Bitcoin, an individual could transfer value to his or her cousin in India without paying a fee to a global money transmitter or a bank for the wire transfer. Though most uses of Bitcoin to make payments will rely on third parties, like Coinbase, Bitcoin may allow these companies to charge lower fees than they do today. This could disrupt the global remit-tance market, valued at $514 billion in 2012, by providing a less expensive method for direct transfers globally.8 Current providers may be forced to lower fees or be replaced by entrants like BitPesa, a mobile payment application for Bitcoin in the developing world.

In the same way that Bitcoin lowers trans-action costs for remittances, it could also lower transaction costs for everyday purchases of low-margin items. Today, if someone buys a donut with a credit card, the merchant pays an interchange fee to the credit card issuer. This interchange fee is usually a small flat amount (10–20 cents) plus a percentage of 1–3 per-cent.9 For a low-margin good like a donut, a 10- to 20-cent flat fee can approach 100 percent of the cost of goods. This interchange fee is often passed on to the customer. Using Bitcoin, the transaction fee could be lowered to as little as 1 percent. This could ultimately evolve into a new payment system for credit card companies and banks.

Transfer of property

The Bitcoin protocol could simplify complex asset transfers, revolutionizing the services that support this industry. Currently, the transfer of large assets requires significant time and resources. For example, in order to purchase a car from an individual seller, one has to engage a third party to transfer the title. Additionally, one has to use services to learn about the car's accident and inspection history. And who doesn't like to spend a Saturday at the Department of Motor Vehicles updating a car registration?

The block chain, Bitcoin's public ledger, could change all of this. Bitcoins can be qualified in such a way that they represent real-world assets. Bitcoin entrepreneurs at companies like Colored Coin are already working on ways to use small portions of Bitcoin to denote physical property. A fraction of a Bitcoin would publicly identify who currently owns that property, and could include a record of both past ownership and other history about the property. When purchasing a car, one would be able to verify all accidents and inspections over the block chain and transfer the title on site. Similarly, real estate and financial instrument transactions could all be executed over Bitcoin or a similar protocol.

This could soon create efficiencies and reduce friction by allowing individuals to directly transfer property without the use of a broker, lawyer, or notary to sign off on the transfer.

Execution of contracts

Bitcoin could similarly be used to structure contracts, bringing new efficiency and transparency to the process. Contracts are typically developed by lawyers on a case-by-case basis, with significant time and resources devoted to negotiation, development, and enforcement. Additionally, markets based on contracts, including certain financial derivatives markets, lack transparency, which complicates regulation.

Traditional contracts could be replaced by code that self-executes when a triggering event occurs. In a simple example, a financial instrument, like an option, could be developed and executed over the block chain. In addition to reducing legal fees, this could bring new transparency to financial markets, as regulators could use the public ledger to understand the market without forcing individual actors to reveal their specific positions. It is possible that new crypto-currencies will emerge to serve these niche purposes.

New ventures, like Ethereum, are creating these capabilities today. Ethereum is developing a network to serve as both the registry and escrow to execute the conditions of a con-tract automatically through rules that can be checked by others.

Identity management

Bitcoin's cryptography and block chain could also transform identity management. Much of identity management, including pass-ports, still operates on a paper-based system. These documents are frequently forged and stolen. Interpol's database currently lists 39 million stolen travel documents. But what if there was a way to create a unique, verifiable key that was impossible to forge?

A cryptographic network similar to but separate from Bitcoin could be used to verify individuals' identities and monitor movement across borders. When a person travels through a checkpoint at a border crossing, instead of showing and scanning a paper passport, he or she could present his or her Bitcoin key. A network privately maintained by the government, a contractor, or other entity could verify the key and register the entry into the ledger. This system, based on cryptography instead of paper documents, would simultaneously increase mobility and security. If Bitcoin can be used for travel documents, it could also be used for other forms of identity management like social security numbers, tax identification numbers, or even driver's licenses.

Property, contracts, and identity management are only a few examples of how a peer-to-peer, open, and frictionless system could change business in the future. In order to achieve this wider adoption, Bitcoin will need to address significant questions around trust, ease of use, and operability. To date, the Bitcoin community has shown remarkable adaptability and it is already working to mitigate these problems. In the next decade, we can expect significant innovation around the Bitcoin network. Though much of that will revolve around payments, particularly early on, the evolution of Bitcoin could take several diverging paths.

FUTURE OF BITCOIN

Many factors will influence Bitcoin's evolution, including regulation, technological innovation, and economic conditions. Predicting the future of

Bitcoin today resembles what it must have been like to try to comprehend the significance of the Internet in the 1990s. Some experts, such as Ray Kurzweil in his book The Age of Intelligent Machines, first published in the late 1980s, got it spectacularly right. But others, like Paul Krugman, who in 1998 predicted that the Internet's impact on the economy would be no greater than the fax machines, were dead wrong, though for understandable reasons. Timelines for the adoption and extension of new technologies are inherently unpredictable, primarily because their ultimate impact will be a result of how humans interact with them.

Bitcoin's future can best be understood by considering four scenarios that represent a range of possible outcomes.

"Life on the fringe"

"Investors flee Bitcoin as another exchange collapse sends bitcoin prices plummeting"

Bitcoin, the currency, never solves its trust and security problems, reinforcing price volatility and skepticism. It remains an arena for illegal activity and speculation. As a result, companies in the Bitcoin ecosystem are unable to enter into mainstream commerce. Exchange collapses and sales of illicit goods and services continue to occur. The majority of bitcoins are held by speculators, crowding out users who want to use the protocol to make legitimate purchases. Bitcoin and its imitators resemble penny stocks instead of a payment system. In short, the focus on bitcoin's obstacles as a cur-rency prevent the benefits of the technology from being fully realized.

How you can tell if this scenario is happening:

• Another exchange meltdown, security breach, or operational failure occurs

• Volatility continues to be 10 to 15 times higher than traditional assets such as gold

• Bitcoin suffers a flash crash

Why this scenario might not happen:

• The Bitcoin community solves the trust and security problems related to bitcoin as currency

• Bitcoin as technology overwhelms the reservations about bitcoin as currency by creating new offerings and markets

What government's role could be:

• Issue guidance and regulations on Bitcoin as a currency and as a technology, signaling that both aspects can be taken seriously

• Focus on enforcement for illicit activity, like money laundering

• Create safeguards to protect mainstream consumers from being victimized by Bitcoin wallet and exchange scams

"CorporateCoin"

"Payment card companies compete to offer low-fee Bitcoin-based payment options"

Payment and technology companies incorporate the Bitcoin protocol into their payment systems. These companies build proprietary payment platforms using cryptography for security and the block chain for transaction validation. Bitcoin moves to the back office and becomes invisible to the consumer in the same way that different Internet protocols are invisible to most web users.

As a result, payments occur across the Bitcoin protocol, but consumers are not required to hold bitcoins. This drives down fees for payment cards and eliminates exchange risk. In short, the Bitcoin protocol grows as a money technology, is adopted by mainstream institutions, and begins to serve as the backbone of many Internet transactions.

How you can tell if this scenario is happening:

• Services offered by traditional payment solutions, like credit and fraud protection, are provided around Bitcoin

• A new wallet technology is introduced in the form of a Bitcoin payment card

Why this scenario might not happen:

• Large payment companies lower fees to match Bitcoin without adopting its protocol

• Corporations continue to distrust open-source technology

What government's role could be:

• Enable companies to use Bitcoin as a payment mechanism through tax and financial crimes enforcement guidance

• Encourage payment companies to use the Bitcoin protocol to offer low-fee solutions for under banked populations

"Satoshi for all"

"Regulators rescuc Wall Street after block chain exposes new market risk"

Bitcoin becomes the protocol for all transfers of value, creating new visibility into financial markets and transforming the services around these functions. Exchanges of value and information, such as property transfer, contract execution, and identity management, are all performed on the block chain. As a result, the services that support these functions are revolutionized. Professionals like traders and lawyers focus on writing code and maintaining the block chain. The process of regulation is changed as well. Regulators download the ledger for a market, such as commodities, every day. Bitcoin's pseudonymity allows regulators to understand the risk of entire markets, while still maintaining the privacy of individual actors. The government creates the Block Chain Administration to oversee cryptographic exchanges and provide consumer protection. In short, all transfers of value are executed in a peer-to-peer and open, yet secure way, reducing fees and increasing transparency.

How you can tell if this scenario is happening:

• A piece of physical property is exchanged over the block chain

• Financial instruments, such as options, are created and traded over the block chain

• A Bitcoin-based central clearinghouse is launched

Why this scenario might not happen:

• Economic path dependence on current sys-tems prevents such significant disruption

• Stakeholder interests challenge adoption

• A Bitcoin programming skills gap expands as the demand for programmers increases

What government's role could be:

• Provide consumer protection and education

• Regulate block chain-based transfers, providing standardization, security, and enforcement

"New networks"

"Number of individuals working 15 or more jobs reaches 10 percent of US population"

Two key attributes of Bitcoin enable a transition to a new model of work and employment. First, Bitcoin's utility in facilitating micropayments allows people to more easily receive compensation for the many tasks they perform as part of a digital network. Second, and perhaps even more important, is that Bitcoin is a self-propelling, decentralized, peer-to-peer network that allows its members to derive both income and utility from their participation. Today's technology services, like email and social media networks, provide utility to users free of charge and generate income for owners. But as the saying goes, if you're getting something for free, you aren't the customer, you're the product. In a Bitcoin world, users are both the customer and the product, because individuals participate in the Bitcoin network by both exchanging the currency and validating the transactions. Currently, at the average day job, a person may spend eight hours at her desk and be paid an income for that one role. In addition, he or she is tweeting, reading news articles, and checking out blogs, generating valuable data throughout the entire day. In the future, we could engage in these same activities and get paid for all of them as Bitcoin enables payment for the myriad activities individuals perform as part of a networked economy.

How you can tell if this scenario is happening:

• Mainstream online media sites reward commenters for input

• A public technology company accounts for user income on its 10-K

Why this scenario might not happen:

• This is a major departure from our current employment model

• Achieving this scenario requires technolog-ical savvy on a larger scale than exists today

What government's role could be:

• Adjust definition of employment to include this new type of work

• Refocus taxation and other policies to stimulate this new type of work

• Tap into the new labor pool created by this employment model

These scenarios lie within the realm of the possible. Though the first scenario is closest to the status quo, current trends may indicate that the second scenario is possible in the near term, which may lay the groundwork for the seemingly more distant scenarios. Certainly, some skeptics argue that Bitcoin will be the Esperanto of finance.13 But, others are intrigued by Bitcoin's potentially more revolutionary impact. As Kevin Kelly, co-founder of Wired, writes in his latest book New Rules for the New Economy, "The great benefits reaped by the new economy in the coming decades will be due in large part to exploring and exploiting the power of decentralized and autonomous networks." Bitcoin is an early example of this future.

Given the spectrum of possible scenarios, the range of actions available to governments and businesses is broad. Some foreign governments have tried to ban Bitcoin by making the exchange of cash for bitcoins illegal. Others have taken a "wait and see" approach, allow-ing the ecosystem around Bitcoin to develop while closely monitoring it. In the United States, government agencies have begun to issue taxation and other guidance, paving the way for entrepreneurs to create a new wave of Bitcoin-related companies and large corporations to engage in the Bitcoin economy.

Bitcoin is yet another example of how new technologies and trends can pop up seemingly out of nowhere, creating problems and opportunities for government as it sorts out how to respond. Most governments chose a hands-off approach to the Internet when it emerged in the 1980s. But the lessons of the Internet should be fair warning that these new technologies can come out of nowhere and change everything. Bitcoin's direct relevance to traditional government domains, such as currency and taxes, merits specific consideration. Given its broad potential impact on activities from contracts to identity management, agencies tasked with diverse operations, from financial markets oversight to border patrol, need to monitor Bitcoin's evolution. Governments need to understand how Bitcoin will evolve in the short term. But even more importantly, they need to explore how the concepts underlying this new technology could intersect with their mission in the future.

CHAPTER 5

TRADING AND SELLING YOUR BITCOIN FOR PROFIT

Trading and selling your bitcoin can be a very profitable activity. You probably know someone or heard about someone who bought bitcoins in the early days when they were worth almost nothing, and ended up selling each bitcoin for thousands of dollars!

Or you may know people who engage in trading bitcoins and are profiting very nicely as well. It might seem easy, but the truth is, trading bitcoins is not for everyone.

Beginners are especially advised to take caution and to be mentally and financially ready before taking the plunge into this exciting high-risk and high-reward world. When trading, it's common sense to follow the 'buy low and sell high' strategy so you can make a profit.

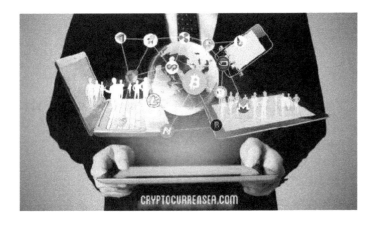

You don't want to sell at a price lower than when you bought in because you'll be selling at a loss. But all these sounds easy on paper.

In the real world, when you're dealing with bitcoins that's worth hundreds, thousands or even millions of dollars, if you don't have the right mindset and the financial discipline, you could panic very easily.

Especially if you're trading bitcoins that represent your entire life savings, your retirement fund, or your kids' college tuition!

Bitcoin Trading Strategies

Common sense and self-control should take precedence over greed and the idea of profiting thousands of dollars in a single day. Here are some bitcoin trading strategies to guide you in the trading world.

Practice First

Learning the ins and outs of bitcoin trading is great, but knowing just theory is different from real-world application. Some bitcoin exchanges offer a demo account where you can play around and experience real-world trading using real-time prices.

You'll get a feel for the landscape, so to speak, and you'll see for yourself whether you've got the stomach for the high-risk game of bitcoin trading.

Plan Your Strategy

To trade bitcoins successfully, you need to have a good strategy in place. You don't just blindly follow the news and think that because everyone's buying bitcoins, then you should be buying too.

Have a plan in place on what price you should buy bitcoins at and what price to sell them at to profit, and make sure you stick to that plan. This means keeping your panic at bay whenever you see the price drop.

Invest Small Amounts

As part of your practice or training strategy, you should start small and don't go all in when you first trade. It is fine to lose all your 'money' in a demo account, but when it's real money, you don't want to risk losing huge sums on your first day.

Control Your Emotions

It's normal to feel alarmed at the first hint of losing your money. However, as you already know Bitcoin is very volatile, and in a single day, the price can go down by hundreds or thousands of dollars. But the opposite is also true. The price can just as easily go up in the next hour or so.

If you keep your emotions in check and think logically, you too can make serious money with Bitcoin trading.

However, if you fail to control your emotions and you let your panic overcome you, then you're bound to lose.

Popular Bitcoin Trading Platforms

Now that you know some very useful Bitcoin trading strategies, it's time to learn about some of the most popular trading platforms for Bitcoin and other cryptocurrencies.

Coinbase

Coinbase is one of the biggest digital currency exchanges in the world today with over 50 billion dollars' worth of digital currency exchanged since 2011. They currently serve more than 10 million customers based in 32 countries.

The platform is very easy to use, and you can easily buy and trade your digital currency.

- To begin, you have to create a free digital wallet which you can use to store your cryptocurrency.

- Next, you need to link your bank account, credit or debit card, so that you can exchange your local currency into the cryptocurrency of your choice.

• Once your account is set up and funded, it's time to buy some crypto.

You have the option to buy bitcoins, ethereum, and litecoin. You can do this either on their website or their handy mobile app.

Now that you've got some bitcoins, you can choose to start trading on Coinbase's GDAX (Global Digital Asset Exchange) trading platform although this is geared towards more advanced and experienced traders.

For beginners though, it's best to stick to Coinbase's more newbie-friendly interface. The good thing about Coinbase is that your digital currency is fully insured while your fiat currency (local currency) are stored in custodial bank accounts. The USD Coinbase wallets of US citizens are covered by FDIC insurance, up to a maximum of $250,000.

To sell your bitcoins, ethereum or litecoins, you simply need to indicate the amount you want to sell and the wallet you're selling from. Then select the linked bank account you wish to deposit your cash to.

At this time, Coinbase does not allow the proceeds of your sale to be sent to a credit or debit card, so it's important you link a bank account to your Coinbase account.

Kraken

Kraken is one of the most trusted names in bitcoin and cryptocurrency exchange since 2011. The company is also considered to be the largest bitcoin exchange in terms of Euro volume and liquidity. In addition to trading bitcoins, they also trade US dollars, Canadian dollars, British pounds and Japanese yen.

Many international users love Kraken because it's very accessible internationally and they support many different types of national currencies and cryptocurrencies.

Kraken offers many options for trading. You can easily trade between any of their 17 supported cryptocurrencies with Euros, USD, CAD, JPY, and GBP. They offer so many possible trading pairs, they have a very long page dedicated just for their fee schedule!

To get started with Kraken, you need to create a free account. After you've verified your account, you can then fund it with cash or cryptocurrency and then place an order to buy bitcoins (or another crypto) on the exchange.

When your order request is fulfilled, you can then withdraw your bitcoins/crypto to your wallet. Their web interface is relatively simple when ordering, however, their trading tools are robust and are great for more advanced users.

To sell bitcoins, you need to send your bitcoins from your wallet to your Kraken account and then create a new order to sell or trade them for any of the available national currencies. Once your order is filled, you can then proceed to withdraw the cash to your linked bank account.

CEX.io

CEX.io is one of the most popular cryptocurrency exchange platforms today with over 1 million active users worldwide. However, the company wasn't originally an exchange; it was actually established in 2013 as the first ever cloud mining provider. While the mining aspect of the business has since been closed, their exchange platform is clearly thriving.

Many users appreciate CEX.io's pricing transparency. If you're buying bitcoins, they make it so easy for you to see how much your $100, $200, $500 or $1000 is going to get you. You can also easily see just how much bitcoin you can buy in British Pound, Euro, and Russian Ruble. The buying price is updated every 120 seconds.

To get started, you need to create an account and add funds to it by using your credit card (you can link any number of credit cards to your account), or you can do a bank transfer, too. They accept USD, EUR, RUB, GBP, or your local currency.

Once the funds are added to your account, you can easily buy bitcoins with 1 click. You then have the option of storing it in your CEX.io wallet, trade it or withdraw to your personal wallet.

Selling bitcoins is also very easy on CEX.io. Simply have the bitcoins in your account, then use their handy buy/sell section for instant cash, or you can place an order in the Trade section of the site (you might get a better exchange rate if you trade).

You can quickly withdraw your earnings to your Visa or Mastercard and receive your funds instantly. Alternatively, for larger transactions, you can withdraw via bank transfer or SEPA if you're in Europe.

Bitstamp

Founded in 2011 in the UK, Bitstamp is one of the pioneers in Bitcoin trading. They are constantly improving their services, and to date, they allow trading of bitcoin, ripple, litecoin, ether and bitcoin cash. Bitstamp has a good reputation worldwide especially since they accept trades from anyone in the world.

All major credit cards are accepted as well, so it makes the platform very friendly to international users. They also promise no hidden fees with transparent volume-based pricing. They guarantee that 98% of digital funds are stored offline for security.

Bitstamp does not sell bitcoins themselves. Instead, they provide a service or platform where people trade directly with each other and buyers get their bitcoins and sellers get their cash at the price they want.

To get started with buying and selling bitcoins, you must create a Bitstamp account. You then need to transfer funds to your account via SEPA, wire transfer or credit card. Once payment is credited, you can place an instant buy order which will allow you to automatically buy bitcoins at the lowest price offered on the Bitstamp market.

A second option to buy bitcoins is by placing a limit order wherein you can set the price you are willing to buy bitcoins.

To sell bitcoins, you need to load your Bitstamp account with bitcoins first. Once you've done this, you can then place an instant sell order to automatically sell your bitcoins at the highest price offered on the market.

Alternatively, you can place a sell limit order where you can set the price at which you are willing to sell your bitcoins. Once your bitcoins are sold, you can proceed to withdraw your funds in USD or EUR currency.

Bitfinex

Since 2014, Hong Kong-based Bitfinex has been the world's largest cryptocurrency trading platform in terms of volume. This full-featured spot trading platform allows trades among the major cryptocurrencies such as Bitcoin, Ethereum, Litecoin, Money, Dash, Ripple, and more. Having such a large volume of Bitcoin exchanges happening on this platform implies the best liquidity.

This means you can trade a large volume of bitcoins at the price you want. Bitfinex's fees are also very low as compared to other cryptocurrency exchanges on this guide. This is why a lot of people like trading on this platform as more money goes to their accounts instead of being paid in fees.

Funding your Bitfinex account is not as simple as the other exchanges though. The only way to deposit money is via bank wire transfer which can take days. On top of the delay, you'd also have to pay Bitfinex a 0.1% of the deposit amount with a $20 minimum. Withdrawing your dollars is also a headache as they only offer bank wire withdrawals. Your money may take up to 7 days to post to your account!

To avoid this inconvenience, trading experts suggest getting your bitcoins or other crypto elsewhere and then just transferring it to your Bitfinex account. For withdrawals, you can withdraw your crypto to your wallet and then sell it locally. This workaround means you just use Bitfinex strictly for trading cryptocurrencies.

Are You Ready To Start Trading Bitcoins?

There are many more bitcoin and cryptocurrency exchanges we've not been able to include in this guide. It's best to perform due diligence and research before selecting a trading platform. Just remember that whichever cryptocurrency exchange platform you choose to do business with, you must always move your cryptocurrency to a more secure wallet such as a hardware wallet or paper wallet.

Don't leave it in your exchange's wallet as it's at great risk of being stolen by hackers. If you must store some in your online wallet, just keep the smallest amount you can afford to lose.

USING BITCOIN AS AN INVESTMENT STRATEGY

Bitcoin is a relatively new form of currency which is just starting to gain traction and worldwide acceptance. With the recent exponential growth in the value of Bitcoin, many people are investing in this digital currency to hopefully reap huge profits in the future.

In this guide, we will cover the basics of using bitcoin as an investment strategy. Note that we are referring to long-term investment here which is not the same as trading bitcoin for short-term profits.

Investing in the highly volatile cryptocurrency market may not seem like such a good idea for some people. Ideally, you'd have nerves of steel, the discipline and focus to ignore short-term gains, as well as the patience to hold your investment until the right time comes.

If you're really determined to own a small share of the crypto-market, then you should at least know the most suitable methods so you can make the most of your investment.

Bitcoin Investment Methods

Dollar Cost Averaging Method

This strategy is best for beginners to the investing world because you don't need to worry about entering the market at the right time.

You don't have to stress yourself waiting for the price of bitcoin to go down; rather, you just buy at regular time intervals to spread the risk and hold/store your bitcoins in a cold, secure wallet (like a paper wallet or hardware wallet).

For example, if you have an extra $100 to spare every week, you can buy bitcoins every week. Some weeks your $100 may buy you more bitcoin, and some weeks the same amount will buy you less.

This method gives you peace of mind because you don't need to worry about the dips in bitcoin price. You just have to be disciplined enough to follow your regular schedule and buy when you need to buy without looking at the bitcoin price charts. You don't wait for the price to go down just because you see a downward trend on the charts, you just go right out and buy your bitcoins.

With the dollar cost averaging method, your profits will also average out when you decide to sell your bitcoins. It might not come anywhere close to profits if you invested using the lump sum method, but if you sell at the right time (when the price is high), you'll still make a healthy profit from your investment.

Lump Sum Investing Method

The lump sum method is a much riskier method of investing bitcoins because you will be buying your bitcoins at a single price point.

If you have $100,000 to invest, you will, of course, want to buy the most number of bitcoins, so you wait for the price to go down. To maximize your investment, you will be compelled to wait for the possible lowest price before buying your bitcoins.

This method means you will have to 'time' the market, so you buy at just the right time. Of course, this is easier said than done with a volatile commodity like bitcoin. The price varies so much it's extremely difficult to predict when the next price dip is so you can buy at that price.

Trying to time the market can cause a lot of headache and stress to an inexperienced investor. It just brings too many 'what ifs' to mind, such as: 'What if I just wait a few more hours, the price may go down, and I'd be able to buy more bitcoins then.' Or 'What if the price never goes down to the price I want to buy bitcoins at, I'll never be able to buy bitcoins.'

When it comes to selling off your lump sum investment in the future, you may find it hard to sell as well because you'll be waiting to sell at the right time so you can make the most profit.

You'll try to predict the highest price point, and you'll berate yourself if you sold too soon and lose out on the possibility of much greater profit.

The good thing with lump sum investment method though is if you manage to buy at the lowest possible price and sell at the highest possible price, then you'll make a much bigger profit than if you invested bitcoins using the dollar cost averaging method.

Crypto Hedge Fund Investing Method

If you don't want to trouble yourself with learning the basics of investing using either the dollar cost averaging method or the lump sum method, you might be better off investing your money in a cryptocurrency hedge fund. However, this option is best suited for people who can afford to pay their hefty management and performance fees.

The management fee is paid upfront; some funds require a 2% management fee so if you're investing $100,000, $2,000 of that is going to the management fee which means only $98,000 will be invested in cryptocurrency.

Also, your hedge fund manager will get a percentage of your profits. Some managers require a 20% performance fee so if you profit $50,000 from your investment, $10,000 of that is going to be paid as an incentive fee.

The hedge fund method may not suit everyone, but if you look beyond the fees, you're at least looking at a hands-off approach to investing which could prove to be very profitable for both you and your hedge fund manager.

Strategies To Succeed In Bitcoin Investing

Investing in bitcoin is similar to investing in stocks. Both are high risk and high reward investments which, undoubtedly, is not for everyone.

Bitcoin is even more volatile than stocks so if you want to invest in this cryptocurrency or any other crypto for that matter, you need to know the following strategies to succeed.

Have A Solid Plan In Place

Don't invest blindly and don't invest just because everyone you know has bought bitcoins. When investing, you need to have a good, solid plan in place where you draw your entry point and your exit point.

Your plan will need to be in accordance with the investment method you'll choose to follow. So if you choose the dollar cost averaging method, you need to have a solid plan like how much and how often you'll be buying bitcoins.

For lump sum investing, you need to know in advance at what price you'll be buying your bitcoins and buy at that price (don't wait for it to go any lower). For hedge fund investing, you need to consider the fees you need to pay and know the best time to invest.

Be Prepared For Volatility

This is the number one strategy you need to master. Everyone knows that bitcoin is a highly volatile investment with prices going up and down by hundreds of dollars in mere minutes. You might think to yourself you already know it's going to be volatile because you've seen the charts and the graphs and you've practiced in a demo bitcoin exchange account.

You can handle the risk, you tell yourself. But when you've got thousands of real dollars on the line, it's a very different scenario. Especially if you've worked hard to get those dollars! You might have worked for it for months or years, and there's a very real chance you could lose it all in just a few minutes.

The best thing you can do is to not bother with the dips at all. Just do something that will help you relax and keep your mind off bitcoins because if you don't, you can literally go crazy. Bitcoin investing is like a roller coaster ride; you just need to hold on really, really tight until you get to the end of the ride!

Keep Calm And Don't Panic

Saying this to panicked investors is very easy, but when you're the panicked one, it's a different feeling altogether. The thought of thousands of dollars down the drain is enough to send anyone to a mental breakdown which would, of course, lead to irrational decisions.

If you don't think clearly, you might think of cutting your losses right there and then without thinking of what's going to happen in the long term. If you played your cards right, your bitcoins would be worth so much more than when you paid for it. But you're never going to experience that if you panic and sell early.

Keep Perspective

Investing in bitcoin is a long-term financial activity. It's different from day-to-day trading which involves a lot more technical analysis so a trader can make a nice profit. When investing in bitcoin, you have zoom out of the bitcoin price charts and look at the overall picture. Don't bother looking at the daily, weekly or monthly charts because it's going to bring you nothing but stress. Look at how far bitcoin rates have come. From literally a few cents when it first started to thousands of dollars now. And experts are saying this upward trend will continue for many more years to come so if you ride out the highs and lows of bitcoin, you'll end up with a very nice investment portfolio in a few years.

Don't Spend What You Can't Lose

This is probably the most important advice you need to take note of. You already know investing in highly volatile cryptocurrencies can either make you insanely rich or bankrupt. But it doesn't have to be these two extremes.

You don't have to invest your entire fortune or your entire life savings in bitcoin or any other cryptocurrency!

The most prudent thing you can do is to only invest what you can afford to lose. This means not spending any money that you cannot afford to lose.

Whether you choose to invest using the dollar cost averaging method, lump sum investing method, or maybe even investing in a crypto hedge fund, don't use money that needs to be used somewhere else.

If you've got money set aside for your retirement, a health fund, an emergency fund, or maybe even your kids' college money, don't even think about touching these funds. So many families have fallen apart because of wrong financial decisions and spent such important funds on risky investments. If you've done something similar in the past and was able to get away with it, that is, you've made some profits, then don't get cocky and think you can do the same with cryptocurrency. It's a different animal, so to speak. It's the

Wild West of investments right now, and you don't want to lose your hard-earned money.

Patience And Discipline Are Keys To Success

Bitcoin investing is a long-term game. You need to be patient when the bitcoin price goes down, and your investment along with it. If you've looked at bitcoin trends, you'll see it's been in an upward trend since its inception in 2009, so you just need to ride out the troughs until you get to the right crest where you'll be happy to sell your bitcoins.

In the world of Bitcoin investing, there'll be many troughs and crests. You just need the discipline to hold on to your investments and not get scared when prices get too low. Likewise, don't get too excited when the price goes up. A solid plan, patience, and discipline will lead you to bitcoin investing success.

Hindsight Is Always 20/20

Don't berate yourself if you bought at a price much higher than the current bitcoin price. And there's no point getting angry at yourself if you sold your bitcoins too early when the price goes up after you sold.

No one can predict the future. So the best thing for you to do is just aim to make a tidy profit and not think about the 'what ifs' because that's really not going to help you at all.

As they say, hindsight is always 20/20. To put things into perspective, if everyone can see the future, we would all have invested in bitcoins when it was first introduced by Bitcoin founder, Satoshi Nakamoto.

Accepting And Using Bitcoin In Your Business

While many online and brick-and-mortar shops and businesses have added Bitcoin to their payment options, it's still not as widespread as the Bitcoin community would like it to be. Most business owners still prefer traditional payment methods as they simply don't know enough about Bitcoin and what they'd get out of adding it to their business.

Many don't trust Bitcoin and its volatility. They're probably thinking that with such volatile changes in the dollar-bitcoin exchange rates, they would probably end up losing their profits. This fear is understandable, but there have been so many innovations nowadays that this really isn't a concern at all.

After all, many well-known companies like Microsoft, Overstock, Expedia, Wikipedia, Wordpress.com, Shopify, and so much more, are already accepting Bitcoin payments.

Online And Offline Businesses Can Accept Bitcoin Payments

Just because Bitcoin is a virtual currency that is electronic in nature doesn't mean that offline shops can't take advantage of receiving bitcoin payments. For online shops, you can integrate payment processors such as Stripe, Coinbase, Braintree, and more, into your e-commerce site's checkout page.

For offline shops, you can choose from Bitcoin terminals or Point-Of-Sale apps such as

XBTerminal, Coinify or Coingate. You can also print out QR codes that your customers can scan with their mobile wallets and easily pay you in bitcoins.

Once your bitcoin wallet is set up, all you have to do is announce to the whole world you're ready to accept Bitcoin payments.

How To Handle The Volatility Of Bitcoin

The thought of losing your profits and essentially giving away your merchandise for free to your customers is one scary thought as you can quickly go bankrupt if all your customers paid in bitcoin.

At one point in time it may have been true, but with Bitcoin payment processors like Coinbase and BitPay, it's now possible to receive your payments in bitcoin and have it instantly converted to US dollars or any other supported currency. This way you avoid all the risks associated with bitcoin and receive the full dollar amount you're supposed to receive.

To illustrate, if your customer pays you $100 worth of bitcoin for a pair of jeans, then you're going to receive exactly $100 in your bank account. The payment gateway you use, for example BitPay, will shield you from bitcoin's volatility so you always get the full dollar amount. For the more enterprising business owners who can handle Bitcoin's unpredictability, the opportunity to make even more profit from the bitcoins they've been paid with might be irresistible.

If you belong to this category, you would probably choose to keep your bitcoins in your digital wallets, and forego the use of a payment processor who will automatically convert your bitcoins to dollars.

Why Your Business Should Start Accepting Bitcoin Payments

Bitcoin was created by Satoshi Nakamoto in response to the 2008 financial market crash which almost crippled the entire global economy. He created it to solve or overcome the problems we have with having a centralized banking system that benefited banks more than they did consumers.

Just think about the bank fees you have to pay everytime someone pays you for your product or service. Deposit fees, withdrawal fees, transaction fees, credit card fees, and all sorts of fees are deducted from your hard-earned money.

Bitcoin's purpose was to avoid all that, and this peer-to-peer electronic cash system was Satoshi Nakamoto's solution to the problem. The system was created essentially so that everyone gets what is due them without the unnecessary intervention of banks and government.

THE BENEFITS OF BITCOIN PAYMENTS FOR YOUR BUSINESS

There are plenty of benefits for your business if you choose to start accepting bitcoin payments. Here are some of them:

No Risk Of Chargebacks

Paypal, credit and debit card payments leave your business vulnerable to chargebacks. Most, if not all, businesses (both online and offline merchants) have probably experienced this problem at one point or another. Dealing with a chargeback is a headache-inducing and time-consuming process.

Your customers can claim to not recognize the charge on their card statements, or their card was stolen and somebody else used it to buy from you, or they're upset that your merchandise was not as described or it was defective.

Some people simply like to do chargebacks because they want to get an item for free, especially if it's a high-value item. Of course, this is a very unethical thing to do, but you can't predict your customers' behaviors.

With Bitcoin payments, there is zero risk of chargebacks because all payments, once it has been confirmed, are final. There is no way for anyone, not even the savviest and smartest programmers in the world, can reverse or undo a bitcoin transaction.

Bitcoin payments offer merchant protection that is unparalleled by any other payment option available today. No bank and no government can give you the level of merchant protection that Bitcoin does.

No Fraud And Double Payments

The Bitcoin network is an extremely secure payment system. Unlike banks, Bitcoin is incorruptible. Before Bitcoin came along, double payments and fraud were a very real problem with digital cash but luckily, thanks to the efforts of Satoshi Nakamoto, the problem of double spending was finally solved.

Bitcoin is a decentralized, peer-to-peer payment system. Everyone on the network sees all the bitcoin transactions that have ever taken place.

This transparency makes it difficult for fraudsters to fake records so they can spend the same amount of bitcoins twice or double spend it.

This massive ledger, also known as the blockchain, keeps a record of all transactions. A transaction is only added to a block once it has been confirmed or verified by miners that the transaction is valid.

Near Instant Payments

Bitcoin payments are fast, irrevocable and final. There's no way for anyone to undo any bitcoin transaction. As long you indicate the correct bitcoin address for your customers to pay into, you're good to go, and your bitcoins will arrive in your wallet usually within 10-45 minutes.

Using the correct bitcoin address is obviously a very important point to consider because if by any chance, you present the wrong bitcoin address, then there's no way for you to recover those bitcoins. Unless of course, you know who owns that bitcoin address, then you can simply ask them to send those bitcoins to your correct address.

Another upside to using payment gateways like Coinbase and BitPay is that you can receive your cash in your bank accounts within 2-3 days. These services usually send payments every business day (not everytime a transaction occurs).

Alternatively, if you want to keep your bitcoins, that is, you don't want to convert them to dollars, then that's perfectly fine. You can select this option in your payment gateway settings. Either way, you're going to get your bitcoins or your dollars very conveniently and in less time than if the customer paid with Paypal or a credit card.

Negligible Transaction Fees

With bitcoin payments, you get to keep more of what your customer pays you. You effectively cut out the middleman (your bank) with their expensive fees. You will still need to pay a very small bitcoin transaction fee which goes to the miners who verify all bitcoin transactions and add it to the ledger or blockchain.

This transaction fee is almost negligible and is a mere equivalent to cents, unlike the fees your bank or credit card company requires you to pay!

For credit card payments, merchants are usually charged an interchange fee (paid to the bank or card issuer) and an assessment fee (paid to the credit card company such as Visa or Mastercard). On average, these fees will end up costing the merchant around 3% to 4% per transaction.

In comparison, for bitcoin transactions, the fees are typically around 10,000 Satoshis or 0.0001 bitcoin. You're free to set your own fees, but the higher the transaction fee you set per transaction, the faster bitcoin miners will confirm your transaction.

For a $1,000 credit card payment, the fees that merchants have to pay would be around $30 to $40. For a similar purchase amount paid for in bitcoin, the transaction fee would roughly be around $1 if the current bitcoin price is say, for example, $10,000 per bitcoin ($10,000 x 0.0001 = $1).

You can already see just by this example that bitcoin transactions will save you a lot of money just in transaction fees. Imagine how much you will get to save if you're able to sell your $1,000 product just 10 times a day or 100 times a day!

Increased Sales And More Profit For You

Bitcoin doesn't discriminate where anyone comes from. Even if your customer lives in a country known for credit card fraud, in Bitcoin's eyes everyone is equal. If you've ever tried to accept payments from customers in these countries, you know just how difficult and cumbersome the entire process is.

Paypal, Stripe and other popular payment gateways don't accept or support many countries with high prevalence of fraud. But with Bitcoin, you can easily accept payments from anyone who lives anywhere in the world. All they need to pay you is just your bitcoin address!

They don't need to send their photos and national ID cards, so your customers' privacy is well protected. And as you already know, all bitcoin transactions are final, so there's no way for any of your customers to do a chargeback like they easily can with a credit card.

Bitcoin makes the world a smaller and better place. It erases borders, government red tape, and bureaucracy. It allows merchants and business owners like you to receive payments from customers who are unfortunate enough to live in countries with a high fraud rate.

Bitcoin protects you and your business. At the same time, it allows you to provide your service and your products to everyone in the whole world.

Happier Customers

Adding Bitcoin to your list of supported payments will give your customers an extra choice to hand over their money to you. Even if they don't have bitcoins yet, they might eventually get into the game sooner or later.

And when they do, they'll remember you and recommend you to their friends. Even existing customers will be happy to know you've added Bitcoin payments.

If you're one of the few businesses in your community that accepts Bitcoin payments, then you're probably going to become popular because you'll be viewed as an innovative and forward-thinking business.

Many people have heard about Bitcoin on the news, and many would have developed a passing interest or have begun to become curious about bitcoins and cryptocurrency in general. You can educate your customers and let them know what Bitcoin is and how it will help them in their financial transactions.

Think about it, would you rather be one of the first businesses to offer Bitcoin payments and steal your competitor's customers in the process? Or would you rather have your customers go to your competition simply because they offer Bitcoin payments, and you don't?

Get Support From The Bitcoin Community

The Bitcoin community is growing fast, and with skyrocketing bitcoin prices, they are looking for places where they can spend their bitcoins. A number of big companies have added Bitcoin to their payment options, but a great majority of businesses have yet to follow suit. So when the Bitcoin community discovers a new business that supports bitcoin, they share the news with everyone. That's free advertisement for your business, and you can expect them to drop by your website or physical store anytime soon.

To get sufficient exposure to the Bitcoin community, you can spread the news on social media, in Bitcoin forums, pages, groups, etc. If you have a physical store, you should also put a large signboard outside that will announce to anyone passing by that you're accepting Bitcoin payments.

Growing your business doesn't have to be difficult. Accepting Bitcoin payments will not only make your business popular among the Bitcoin community, but it will also lead to more sales and more profits for you.

How To Protect Yourself Against Fraud And Theft

Bitcoin and cryptocurrencies are hot commodities right now. Everyone wants a piece of the action, though with soaring prices, many can't afford to buy and invest out of their own pockets.

So they do the next best thing they can think of – scam and steal these precious digital coins from other people. In this guide, we'll show you some of the most common scams these con artists are running as well as how you can protect yourself against them.

BITCOIN AND CRYPTOCURRENCIES ARE NOT SCAMS

Before we go into the main scams you should be aware of, we'd like to point out that these scams are all from outside forces, and not cryptocurrencies themselves. You might hear some people say that cryptocurrencies are nothing but a huge scam but it's 100% false, and we'll explain why.

The technology behind cryptocurrencies is called the blockchain. It is an incorruptible digital ledger that records all transactions in the network. No central body controls it. It is transparent, and anyone can track any transaction that has ever happened in the past.

No one can alter any transaction recorded on the blockchain because doing so would mean you'd have to alter the rest of the transactions or blocks that came after that particular transaction; this is virtually an impossible task to do.

The blockchain is so secure that many banks and startup companies are now experimenting, and starting to implement blockchain technology because they've seen just how well it works on Bitcoin and cryptocurrencies.

Now that you know you can trust the technology behind cryptocurrencies, let's discuss the most common scams that many people fall prey to.

Scam #1 – Fake Bitcoin Exchanges

There are plenty of reputable bitcoin exchanges today. The biggest and most popular platforms that have been around a few years are Coinbase, Kraken, CEX.io, Changelly, Bitstamp, Poloniex, and Bitfinex. With that being said, we cannot vouch for any company even if they're well known in the industry.

You will have to do your due diligence by researching the company's history, user reviews, and determine for yourself whether you want to spend your hard-earned fiat money with them.

Too Good To Be True Exchange Rates

Due to the highly volatile nature of cryptocurrencies (prices can go up and down by a huge spread in just a few hours!), many unsavory characters on the Internet are capitalizing on this volatility. They prey on unsuspecting beginners who can't spot the difference between a legitimate exchange and a fake one.

These fake bitcoin exchanges can easily put up nice-looking websites and impress people with their seemingly sophisticated look. They hook people in with their promises of lower-than-market-rate prices and guaranteed returns. Simply put, they play on people's greed.

Imagine how ecstatic you'd feel if you found out about a website that offers bitcoins at 10% or 20% lower rates than the going rates on Coinbase or Kraken. If these large platforms are offering $15,000 for 1 bitcoin, and this other site is offering it at $12,000, wouldn't you jump at the chance?

You'd save so much ($3,000 per bitcoin!), and you can use your savings to buy even more bitcoins. See, that's them playing on greed! They know that people want to buy more bitcoins for less dollars. And who can blame those poor victims? If we didn't know any better, we might fall for the same scam too.

Receive Instant PayPal Payment For Your Bitcoins

Another method these fake bitcoin exchanges use to steal your bitcoins is they'll offer to buy your coins at higher-than-market-rates, and then send the equivalent dollar amount to your PayPal address.

To the unsuspecting bitcoin owner, he thinks he's getting the better end of the deal because he's going to get more money for his bitcoins, and he'll get the cash instantly in his PayPal account.

So, he enters the amount of bitcoins he wants to sell, confirms he's happy with the equivalent dollar amount, types in his PayPal address so they can send the money to him, then he waits. And waits. And waits some more.

He'll contact the website but, of course, they're not going to reply to him now because they have his bitcoins (remember, all bitcoin transactions are final and irreversible once validated).

At this point, he'll realize he's just been scammed. He can report the site and write bad reviews, but who's he kidding? These savvy scammers will just set up shop under a new domain name and wait for their next victim.

The key takeaway here is to stay away from 'exchanges' with too-good-to-be-true rates. As the saying goes, if it's too good to be true, it probably is.

Scam #2 – Phishing Scams

There are so many kinds of phishing scams that run rampant today. Ever received an email from your 'bank' asking you verify or update your account details to make sure your details remain up to date? And that you have to click on the email link to update your details?

Many people are aware these types of emails are nothing more than a scam. Modern email services send these junk emails to the junk folder anyway, so you don't see them all that much nowadays.

But with Bitcoin and cryptocurrency being so new and so hot in the news right now, scammers are scrambling to find a way to steal your bitcoins by getting access to your digital wallets!

Email Phishing Scams

Scammers will send you an email designed to make it look like it came from your online wallet service (this is why we don't suggest storing large sums of virtual currency in your exchange wallets).

In the email, they'll ask you to click on a link which will lead you to a fake website. It will look exactly like your exchange or wallet website. Of course, it's not the same because the domain name will be different.

For example, if you're using Coinbase, they'll use a similar misspelled domain such as:

- Cooinbase
- Coiinbase
- Coinbasse
- Coinsbase
- Coinbase-Client-Update.com
- or something similar...

It will also most probably not have a security feature called SSL installed, which means the domain will start with HTTP and not HTTPS (modern browsers like Chrome and Firefox should warn you if it's a secure site or not).

If you fall for this phishing scam, and you log in to the fake wallet site, then the scammers now have your login details to your real wallet! They can easily lock you out of your account, and they'll then have the freedom to transfer every single bitcoin you own to their own wallets.

Malware Scams

In this type of scam, scammers will ask you to click on a link either via email, banner ad, forum ad, or anywhere they can post a link which will then download a type of malware to your computer.

Often, these malwares are keyloggers which will record everything you type on your computer, and send the information to the scammers. So, if you log in to your online wallet, like Coinbase for example, they will be able to see your username and your password, and they can then log in to your account and easily steal your coins from you!

The key takeaway for protecting yourself from these types of scams is to never click on links from untrustworthy sources.

If you don't recognize the sender, or the website domain name is misspelled, it should raise a red flag, and you should report the email and/or leave the phishing site right away.

Furthermore, consider using offline storing methods such as paper wallets or hardware wallets so even if scammers get access to your online wallet, they'll have nothing to steal there.

Scam #3 – Cloud Mining Scams

Cloud mining is a popular way of becoming a bitcoin miner. You no longer need to invest in your own supercomputer and join a mining group to solve complex cryptographic hash problems. You don't even need to worry about expensive electricity bills.

You simply need to sign up to a cloud mining service (also known as a mining farm), rent mining equipment, and receive payments proportionate to your subscription.

While some cloud mining companies are legitimate, there are many fly-by-night websites which promise unrealistic returns for measly sums, whose sole purpose is to steal your money.

Some common red flags to watch out for when looking to join a cloud mining service is the absence of an About page, Terms of Use/Service page, physical address, and/or contact number.

They might also not have a secure domain (no HTTPS before their domain name). These details are all very important in figuring out which site is a scam and which is not. You can search Google for reviews and go through their website to get a feel if they're legitimate or not. More often than not, these sites would be anonymous with no names or faces behind them.

Some may appear legitimate at first but take a deeper look at what your investment's going to get you. You may pay eventually sign up for a contract which is going to cost you a few thousand dollars a year but what are you going to get in return? You'll have to do the math yourself and calculate if you're going to end up in the green.

The key takeaway here is before you spend any of your hard-earned fiat money, you should at least make sure you're dealing with a legitimate company and not some anonymous scammer who'll leave you in tears.

Do plenty of research, read reviews, and browse the crypto-mining communities for information on the best and most trustworthy cloud mining companies.

Scam #4 – Ponzi Scams

Ponzi scams are probably easier to spot than the other scams we've covered so far in this guide. This is because Ponzi scams are well known for guaranteeing outlandish returns on investments with little to no risk to the investors. People fall for these sorts of scams all the time because people want guaranteed returns on their investments.

With Bitcoin and cryptocurrency, any company that guarantees exponential returns on any investment should be viewed as a potential scammer. The cryptocurrency market is highly volatile, and one minute the price could be at an all-time high and the next, it's down by a few hundred or a few thousand dollars.

Because of this volatility, you should never believe anyone who tells you you're guaranteed a 10% return on your investment every single day, or whatever the scammer's terms may be.

Since Ponzi schemes rely on new members, a.k.a. victims, to pay off their early investors, they usually offer incentives for members to recruit new people to join their network.

It's very common for scams like this to offer some form of affiliate rewards. You refer someone to invest in the 'company,' and you get compensated for your efforts.

Some Ponzi schemes guarantee daily profits forever. If this seems impossible, it most certainly is. No one even knows if bitcoins will be around that long and guaranteeing daily returns is just crazy. Right off the bat, an intelligent investor will see that offers like these are nothing more than scams designed to rip you off your money or your bitcoins.

In fact, many of these scam sites prefer bitcoin payments because they know Bitcoin transactions can't be reversed or canceled once sent! Either way, whether they require fiat or cryptocurrency, know who you're sending your money to first.

The key takeaway here is if you know the company's offers are too good to be true, then you should run away in the opposite direction. Sometimes, there's just no point in even looking up reviews on the Internet when it comes to scams like these because most 'reviewers' are those who got in the game early and thus have already received some return on their investment.

And usually, when these users leave reviews they'll include their affiliate link so you know right away they have a vested interest for leaving glowing reviews for a company they may, or may not know, is a scam.

THE FUTURE OF CRYPTOCURRENCY

Cryptocurrency can face good and bad changes in the near future just like any other technology innovation. Some said that due to its volatility, a computer crash can turn the precious virtual coins into bubbles, while some expect the value to rich billions of dollars. Since cryptocurrency has no government and rules to follow we cannot say that is perfectly safe because of its anonymity when it comes to transactions mad. As there are no rules and security from the government, cryptocurrencies are more prone to hacking attacks and fraud.

If you're an individual who wants to invest with these virtual currencies with high risk of volatility, make sure to invest the amount that your pocket can lose. As there was no assurance if in the next days or even seconds, the value of your investment still remain the same. Maybe you can be as lucky as the person who accepted bitcoin as in exchange of pizza, but there is always a possibility of losing all your investment in just a wink of an eye.

Bitcoin, the most popular cryptocurrency already has a good prediction from some enthusiast. Some says that it will surpass into $100,000 in the mid of 2018, while other prediction says that this will be the year where bitcoin soar to drop.

1. Bitcoin	$10,757.00
2. Ethereum	$896.26
3. Ripple	$0.971487
4. Litecoin	$224.21
5. Neo	$142.85
6. Monero	$306.91
7. Cardano	$0.339653
8. Stellar	$3.60

9. TRON	$0.042737
10. Zcash	$ 417.53
11. IOTA	$1.92
12. Dash	$ 643.23

Before we talk about the future of cryptocurrency, it's important to remind ourselves of the past and what cryptocurrency was like in the beginning. Back in 2008, when Bitcoin founder, Satoshi Nakamoto, first released his whitepaper on Bitcoin, many people said it was just a fad and a scam designed to trick people into giving up their 'real' money.

There were many naysayers and financial experts who said Bitcoin will never be adopted by the masses and will fizzle and die out in a year or so. Fortunately, the cryptocurrency community rallied and worked together to make Bitcoin a success. They saw potential in the blockchain technology and what it could mean for the finance sector. They saw the need for cryptocurrency because the current financial setup via banks and governments had too many problems and was causing national economies to collapse.

They saw that keeping inflation at bay was difficult with traditional currencies and the poorest people often have no easy access to banks. Receiving or sending payments was oftentimes a headache with transaction fees eating up a significant amount of money.

Banks charge exorbitant fees just so their customers can get access to their very own money, and the government takes very little action, if at all, to help the people.

Bitcoin supporters say the modern financial system is a mess where banks and governments collude or work together, not to help their citizens' financial needs, but to take as much money as they can from them in terms of fees collected.

Bitcoin changed all that. With Bitcoin, you're cutting out the middleman. There are no more banks to deal with and no government to spy on your bank accounts. With Bitcoin, you are your own bank. You're the bank teller sending and receiving payments, and you're the banker in charge of keeping your money safe.

Bitcoin has been a leader on so many fronts. As the first successful cryptocurrency, it has paved the way for other cryptocurrencies to succeed and the global community has slowly taken notice these past few years. Read on to find out what other possibilities Bitcoin and cryptocurrencies bring for the future!

Massive Support From The Masses

In most developed countries, getting a credit card or a business loan is relatively easy. However, in developing countries, you'd have to literally jump through hoops and government red tape before you can get one. But with Bitcoin and cryptocurrency, all you need is just your digital wallet, and you can start receiving cryptocurrency from anyone, anywhere in the world.

You don't even need your own Internet connection at home; you can simply go somewhere with good Internet access and create a quick wallet online or on your mobile phone. Of course, storing your crypto online is not a good idea so you should look into storing these in cold storage, such as a hardware wallet or paper wallet.

But online wallets are great for small transactions so if you need to pay a utility bill or your credit card bill, simply scan the utility company's bitcoin wallet's QR code and send your crypto payment. No need to spend the whole day standing in long lines!

Today, there are already many businesses which have started to accept bitcoin payments (though they are still in the minority). These forward-thinking business owners see the benefit of accepting bitcoins and are profiting nicely from this smart business decision!

You can buy virtually anything with bitcoins. You can buy plane tickets, you can rent cars, you can pay for your college tuition, you can buy groceries, you can buy stuff on Amazon by purchasing

Amazon gift cards on third-party sites, and so much more!

In the future, we can expect so many more businesses to jump onto the bitcoin payment wagon, and it would be a win-win situation for both business owners and customers.

Businesses will get their payment fast and into their bank accounts the very next day (using a payment gateway like BitPay which offers instant bitcoins to fiat currency conversion), and customers will get to buy items in a very convenient manner.

Bitcoin In Developing Economies

It's not surprising that Bitcoin has seen massive adoption in recent years. In fact, in Zimbabwe, people are using bitcoins to make financial transactions. With the demise of the Zimbabwean dollar, the country had to resort to using US dollars as their main currency.

However, this is not a very feasible solution because their government can't print US dollars themselves. Venezuelans are also experiencing the same problem. The Venezuelan bolivar has become so hyper-inflated it's almost unusable. People have resorted to using bitcoins to pay for basic goods, medicines, groceries, and so much more.

For the Zimbabweans and Venezuelans, as well as the Vietnamese, Colombians, and citizens of countries with super inflated currencies, Bitcoin is a beacon of light because it's not subject to the whims and manipulations of their local banks or their governments.

Their present economic situation is a perfect example of the downside of having a central authority to manage a country's currency, while at the same time, it highlights all the benefits of using Bitcoin, a decentralized and 100% transparent financial network.

With Bitcoin getting massive support from people in developing countries, governments may soon be stepping in to regulate the use of Bitcoin and other cryptocurrencies. While we can't predict the future, for now, Bitcoin provides a wonderful inflation-less alternative to traditional currency.

And with skyrocketing Bitcoin and cryptocurrency prices, this gives many people a lot of purchasing power which their national currencies can't provide.

Fast And Cheap International Payments

One of the main benefits of bitcoin payments is the speed by which the recipient can get their bitcoins. This is perfect for people who hire freelancers or employees overseas.

The employees don't need to sign up for a bank account and incur fees left and right just because they're receiving money from yourself, an international client. Of course, we must not fail to mention the fees that you yourself will be paying to your bank everytime you remit or transfer monies to your overseas workers.

In addition to the fees both you and your recipient pay, you'd also have to factor in the exchange rate. Most banks and money transfer services will usually tell you up front that "this" is the current exchange rate but when you compare it to actual rates, the bank rate would be much lower.

Even for Paypal payments, you'll notice a difference in the exchange rate they use. You probably won't notice the exchange rate when you're transferring relatively small amounts, but when you're transacting in thousands of dollars, the fees can very quickly add up to a significant amount.

With Bitcoin, you can say goodbye to all these exorbitant fees.

For every bitcoin transaction, you do need to pay a small fee for the miners, but it's literally nothing compared to what your banks are charging you! Whether you're sending 1,000 bitcoins or 0.01 bitcoins, the mining fee can be the same since the fee is computed in terms of bytes, not the amount of bitcoins.

The size (in bytes) of your transaction will depend on the number of inputs and outputs per transaction. Without going into the technical details, what's important to take note here is the mining fees are very, very small compared to your bank's fees. This is why Bitcoin and cryptocurrency are going to change the future. More people will transact with each other directly to avoid paying those very expensive bank fees!

With more and more people sending cryptocurrency to each other directly, there may be no more need for third-party money transfer services or even banks. Though this may take many years to happen, it's still a possibility once everyone gets educated on the benefits of using cryptocurrency to send and receive payments from anyone in the world in just a few minutes.

Combat Crime and Corruption

Many people are worried that the Bitcoin network is being used by money launderers, criminals, and corrupt officials because they think it's an anonymous network. Yes, all verified transactions are recorded on the blockchain and no, there are no names listed there.

You can see only alphanumeric codes, lots of it in fact. If you download the free and open source Bitcoin Core client, you'll also need to download the entire blockchain which is already more than

100GB+. Millions of bitcoin transactions since 2009 are stored on the blockchain. You'll even see the first ever transaction by its founder, Satoshi Nakamoto.

We're mentioning this to point to the fact that Bitcoin is not really anonymous. Instead, it's pseudonymous, meaning users can hide behind pseudonyms, but on close inspection, digital forensics experts can trace who owns Bitcoin wallets.

This is, of course, a time-consuming endeavor but when you're after criminals who've laundered millions or billions of dollars' worth of bitcoins then catching them becomes a top priority. In fact, experts say that criminals are better off stashing their stolen loot in offshore bank accounts with their super strict bank privacy laws.

But bitcoin is easier to move around so people think they can easily hide their illicit transactions in the alphanumeric maze known as the blockchain. In short, a number of criminals have been put behind bars thanks to Bitcoin and the blockchain.

In the future, if and when cryptocurrency gains massive support and adoption from the masses worldwide, it will be easier for authorities to trace and catch criminals hoping to use cryptocurrencies as a means to hide and move their stolen money around.

BLOCKCHAIN TECHNOLOGY WILL BECOME MAINSTREAM

Many governments, banks, and private organizations are looking into adopting the blockchain technology into their products and services. The blockchain is the underlying technology behind Bitcoin and other cryptocurrencies.

The technology is already starting to receive recognition and adoption from many sectors in the world. While this may take several years, it's at least a positive nod in favor of the blockchain revolution.

Two of the most popular blockchain technologies today are Ethereum and Hyperledger. You may have heard of Ethereum as the second most popular cryptocurrency, after Bitcoin. But it's more than just a virtual currency platform.

Ethereum is a platform that allows anyone to create smart contracts which help people trade or exchange anything of value, such as money, property, stocks, etc. The contract is publicly transparent and is recorded on the blockchain

188

which means other people are witness to the agreement.

The best thing about smart contracts is you are basically automating contracts without paying for the services of a middleman such as a bank, stockbroker, or lawyer.

Hyperledger, on the other hand, is an open source, cross-industry collaborative project with contributors from many major companies such as Deutsche Bank, IBM, Airbus and SAP.

According to their website, the collaboration aims to develop a "new generation of transactional applications that establish trust, accountability and transparency." These applications have the potential to streamline business processes and reduce the cost and complexity of various systems in the real world.

These are just a few examples of how blockchain technology is going to change the world in the future. Blockchain may be less than a decade old, but it has already changed the lives of so many people for the better.

Will You Be A Part Of Cryptocurrency Revolution?

In this guide, you've learned so many benefits of using Bitcoin, cryptocurrency and blockchain technology. Investing in cryptocurrency may be in your best interest though it's always best to do in-depth research on which cryptocurrency to invest in.

Bitcoin may be too expensive for now but remember that you don't have to buy a whole bitcoin. Alternatively, there are other emerging cryptocurrencies with good track records you may consider investing in.

With cryptocurrency looking set to get integrated with mainstream financial markets, investing in cryptocurrency is not a scary thought anymore. In fact, it just might be the best financial decision you'll ever make for yourself and your family's future.

CONCLUSION

Bitcoins are a new revolutionary currency with tremendous utility. Over the past year there have been significant innovations making simple secure online storage along with quick and easy acquisition of bitcoins possible. Many merchants are accepting bitcoins and you can effortlessly convert them into national fiat currency.

The real speculative and investment excitement is with the developing capital markets within the Bitcoin economy and outrageous cash-on-cash returns currently being generated there and with private lending.

Why not begin experimenting with this innovation to see whether the Bitcoin economy provides you any utility? Paying anonymously for the Private Internet Access's VPN service is a great first purchase.

After all, with the worldwide monetary and financial system in commotion we see with the

Bitcoin economy that monetary innovation is in forward motion like never before. There will be a solution to this gigantic mess and the innovators and creative destroyers will stand to reap tremendous profit. There is a chance that Bitcoin will play a significant role.

With governments engaged in massive quantitative easing, currency controls and intrusive privacy destroying legislation like FACTA then what are your options?

Have you ever thought or taken action to answer the question: If you had to take the last plane out of your country then (1) where would you go and (2) how would you maintain your standard of living?

Bitcoin could very well be your perfect last plane account. There are currently hundreds of thousands of people regularly using it around the globe, wallets cannot be frozen, there are no arbitrary limits and your wealth can, unlike physical gold, easily cross borders as it can exist as nothing but a brainwallet with nothing to declare or have seized at customs.

ABOUT THE AUTHOR

Sir Patrick writes for the liberation of all people, focusing on the beautiful people who are often left out of cryptocurrency and the Bitcoin world. He is an Investment banker and Fund Manager. In addition to that, he is a senior banking redemption officer and Judge for the International Court of Justice.

Thank you again for purchasing this book, I hope you have enjoyed it!

Author: **SIR DR PATRICK BIJOU**.

REFERENCES

Altshuler, Yaniv, Yuval Elovici, Armin B. Cremers, Nadav Aharony, and Alex Pentland.

Security and Privacy in Social Networks. New York City: Springer, 2013.

Britannica Educational Publishing. Economics: Taking the Mystery Out of Money; Money

and Capital. New York City: Britannica Educational Publishing, 2013.

Faktor, Steve. Econovation: The Red, White and Blue Pill for Arousing Innovation. Hoboken:

Wiley, 2011.

Menger, Carl. Principles of Economics. Auburn: Ludwig von Mises Institute, 1976.

Mint, David. Bitcoins: What They Are and How to Use Them. Portland: The Wilcox Trading Company, 2013.

Mises, Ludwig von. The Theory of Money and Credit. New Haven: Yale University Press, 1953.

Sassower, Raphael. Digital Exposure: Postmodern Postcapitalism. Basingstoke: Palgrave

Pivot, 2013.

Singh, Supriya. Globalization. Blue Ridge Summit: Rowman & Littlefield Publishers, 2013.

Szczepankiewicz, Maciej. Money Innovation. Alternative and Complementary Forms of Money in the World. College Park: Maryland UN Publishing, 2013.